JOHN W. SCHAUM PIANO COURSE
A – THE RED BOOK

Leading to Mastery of the Instrument

ITS OBJECTS

1. TO TEACH PIANO in the most natural and enjoyable way.
2. TO PRESENT technical information accurately and progressively.
3. NOT TO DEFINE the scope of Grade I – or Grade II – or any other grades.
4. NOT TO CONFINE the intellectual range of the pupil within the first year or any other period of time.
5. BUT TO OFFER a gradual and progressive pedagogic continuity through a series of books named Pre-A – A – B – C – D – etc.
6. TO LEAD with the assistance of the teacher to eventual mastery of the instrument.

Please particularly note that the division of the books is not based on a definite interpretation or separation of the various grades. Neither did Mr. Schaum attempt to define how much the mind of a pupil is capable of absorbing within a certain period of time.

Progressive Succession of the JOHN W. SCHAUM PIANO COURSE

Pre-A – For the Earliest Beginner
A – The RED Book – Grade 1*
B – The BLUE Book – Grade 1½
C – The PURPLE Book – Grade 2
D – The ORANGE Book – Grade 2½

E – The VIOLET Book – Grade 3
F – The BROWN Book – Grade 4
G – The AMBER Book – Grade 5
H – The GREY Book – Grade 6

*Grades are listed to serve as an approximate guide to the teacher

This revision: Wesley Schaum

Text illustrations: Jeannette Aquino

© 1945 (Renewed), 1996 BELWIN-MILLS PUBLISHING CORP.
All Rights Assigned to and Controlled by ALFRED PUBLISHING CO., INC.
All Rights Reserved including Public Performance

Any duplication, adaptation or arrangement of the compositions
contained in this collection requires the written consent of the Publisher.
No part of this book may be photocopied or reproduced in any way without permission.
Unauthorized uses are an infringement of the U.S. Copyright Act and are punishable by law.

CONTENTS

	PAGE
Foreword	2
Outlining Hands (Correlating fingers with staff names)	3
Sight Reading Discovery	4
Sight Reading Drills	5
Five-finger Position in C Major – *The Woodchuck*	6
Phrase Development – *Snug as a Bug in a Rug*	7
How To Count – *Hannah from Montana*	8
Rhythmic Development – *Crunchy Flakes*	9
Musical Terms – *Swinging Along*	10
Half Steps and Whole Steps (Sharps, Flats and Naturals)	12
Accidentals – *Tick-Tack-Toe*	13
Five-finger Position in G Major – *A Nutty Song*	14
Crescendo and Diminuendo – How to Transpose *Down in a Coal Mine*	15
Andante and Review – *The Kangarooster*	16
Music Appreciation - Beethoven *Bells Are Ringing*	17
Arm Phrasing Touch – *Steady Eddie*	18
Bringing Out the Melody – *The Goofy Gopher*	19
Extended Right Hand Position – *The Dandy Lion*	20
Left Hand Development – *Captain Silver*	21
Piano Quiz No. 1	22
Transposing – *Jumping Beans*	23
Technique – *Warm-Ups*	24
Memorization – *The Snake Dance*	25
Major Scale Pattern Scale Writing	26

	PAGE
C Major Scale (Ascending) – *The Escalator*	27
Broken Chords and the Triad – *The Sphinx*	28
Five-finger Position in F Major *Tune of the Tuna Fish*	29
Extended R.H. Position in F Major *Which is Witch?*	30
Contrast in Music Reading Notes as Well as Finger Numbers *Brahms' Lullaby*	31
A Recital Piece Left Hand Accompaniment Patterns *Riding on a Mule*	32
Five-finger Position in D Major – *Cycles*	34
Common Time Extended R.H. Position in D Major – *The Movies*	35
Intervals: The Third – *At the Ice Cream Counter*	36
New Hand Position (B-flat Major) – *The Picnic*	37
The Pianoforte and Fortissimo – *The Life Guard*	38
Staccato Study – *The Steam Iron*	39
Hand Position: Key of A Major – *The Pet Shop*	40
Repertoire – *The Rodeo*	42
The Dotted Quarter Note in $\frac{4}{4}$ Time *Motorcycle Police*	43
The Dotted Quarter Note in $\frac{3}{4}$ Time *Schubert's Waltz*	44
Reversible Melody – *A Musical Trick The Cheerleader*	45
Changing Keys – *Birthday Greetings*	46
Piano Quiz No. 2	47
Certificate of Promotion	48

Advantage of Supplementary Sheet Music

The pupil gets a glow of achievement and completion from supplementary sheet music. When he or she learns a piece, A WHOLE UNIT is completed. This makes the pupil feel successful, and a successful pupil likes music.

OUTLINING THE HANDS

In the space below trace around the student's left hand and label the fingers according to names of lines and spaces of the bass clef.

In the space below trace around the student's right hand and label the fingers according to names of lines and spaces of the treble clef.

Note: Point out to the pupil that the first line for the R.H. (E) is just a skip away from Middle C. Also, the top or 5th line for the L.H. (A) is a skip away from C.

SCHAUM'S SIGHT READING DISCOVERY

Once there was a famous basketball coach who fastened a smaller size metal ring inside the regulation baskets of his gymnasium. He reasoned that if his team could shoot baskets in the small size rings, then the larger official size baskets would be simple by comparison. His idea worked wonders. His team won the majority of their games.

The same idea works wonders in sight reading. Instead of drilling students on oversized flash cards and then having to read smaller sized notes in actual music — DRILL THE PUPILS ON SMALLER SIZED NOTES SO THAT THE ACTUAL MUSIC IS LARGER AND EASIER BY COMPARISON. The sight reading drills that follow are based on this discovery.

These drills should be done for 1 to 4 minutes of every lesson, until this book is finished. Remember, most often a pupil's difficulty is not because of technic deficiency but is due to weak note recognition. The student stumbles at the keyboard because he/she can't find the notes quickly enough. Consistent use of these drills will help your student to become a good note reader. Parents should be encouraged to practice these drills daily with their child. This will help reinforce note recognition between lessons.

AN EYE SPECIALIST SPEAKS

A famous eye specialist was asked his opinion of this sight reading discovery. Here's what the doctor had to say:

1. "The small size drill card will sharpen the student's vision and tend to make him more accurate."
2. "The student will concentrate more on the small size card. On the large size card, the pupil is inclined toward visual laziness."

The size of the drill card on the following page has been constructed according to scientific measurement. If the student's vision is normal, he or she should be able to do the drills at a distance of 28 inches.

The physical element of good vision is an important factor in sight reading. The teacher should watch the pupil's vision. If a visual problem is suspected, the pupil should be advised to consult an eye specialist.

SIGHT READING DRILLS

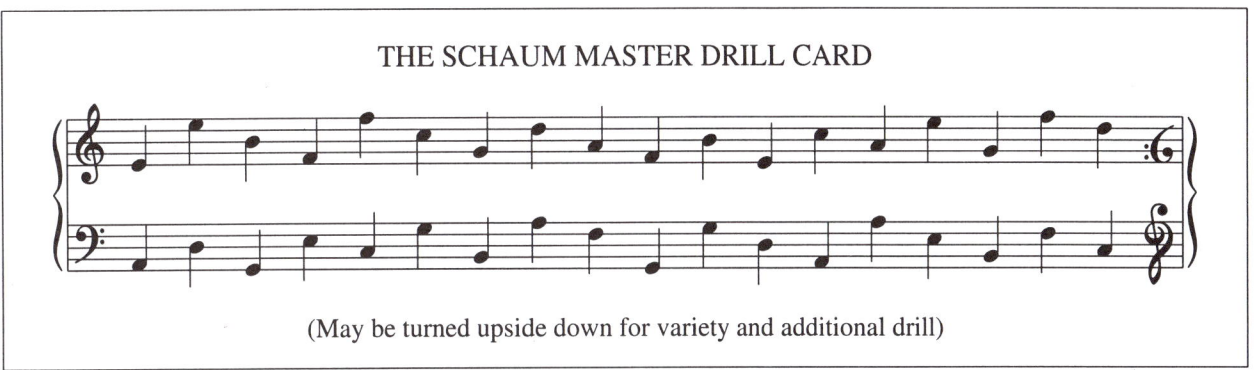

THE SCHAUM MASTER DRILL CARD

(May be turned upside down for variety and additional drill)

Use the Master Card with Each Drill

FIRST DRILL
(Distinguishing Lines from Spaces)

As the teacher points to the notes on the Master Drill Card, the pupil says aloud whether the note is on a line or in a space. It is not necessary to do the entire drill at the lesson; spot-checking may be done to save time. No letter names are mentioned. The student simply says "space" or "line."

SECOND DRILL
(Learning Line and Space Numbers)

This time the pupil says "first line" or "fourth space" as the teacher points to each note on the Master Drill Card. No letter names are mentioned. (Lines and spaces are always counted up from the bottom of the staff.)

THIRD DRILL
(Letter Names of Treble Spaces)

The four spaces of the treble staff spell the word "F-A-C-E." The teacher points to the treble space notes on the Drill Card as the pupil recites the letter names.

F A C E

FOURTH DRILL
(Playing Treble Space Notes on the Piano)

As the teacher points them out, the pupil plays the treble space notes on the piano without looking at the hands if possible.

FIFTH DRILL
(Letter Names of Treble Lines)

The five lines of the treble clef can be remembered by the slogan "Every Good Bird Does Fly." The pupil recites the letter names of the treble lines as they are pointed out by the teacher.

E G B D F

SIXTH DRILL
(Playing Treble Line Notes on the Piano)

The pupil plays the treble line notes on the piano without looking at the hands if possible.

SEVENTH DRILL
(Combining Letter Names of Treble Spaces and Lines)

Same procedure as in the Fifth Drill but here the pupil recites the letter names of both lines and spaces.

EIGHTH DRILL
(Playing Treble Line and Space Notes on the Piano)

NINTH DRILL
(Learning Letter Names of Bass Spaces)

The slogan "All Cars Eat Gas" will help in remembering the four bass spaces. The pupil recites the bass clef space notes as they are pointed out on the Master Drill Card.

A C E G

TENTH DRILL
(Playing Bass Space Notes on the Piano)

The pupil plays the bass space notes on the piano trying not to look at his or her hands.

ELEVENTH DRILL
(Learning Letter Names of Bass Lines)

The slogan "Great Big Dogs Fight Animals" will help in remembering the names of the five bass clef lines. The pupil recites the letter names of the five bass clef lines as they are pointed out on the Drill Card.

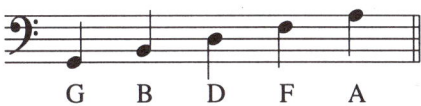

G B D F A

TWELFTH DRILL
(Playing Bass Line Notes on the Piano)

The pupil plays the bass line notes on the piano trying not to look at his hands.

THIRTEENTH DRILL
(Reciting Letter Names of Bass Lines and Spaces)

FOURTEENTH DRILL
(Playing Bass Lines and Spaces on the Piano)

EL00166A

Place the hands over the keys as shown in the hand position chart. Then play the preparatory drill several times. Keep your hands in this position when you play "The Woodchuck."

1. THE WOODCHUCK

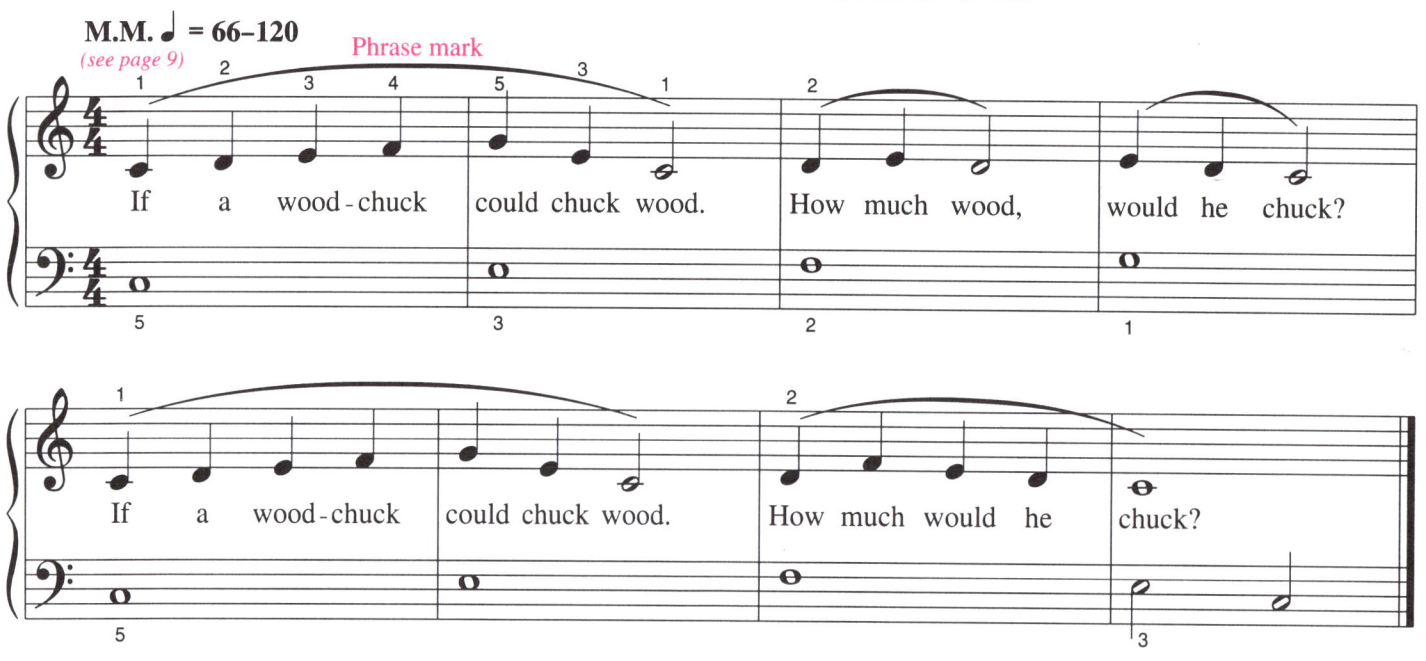

EXPRESSION IN MUSIC

The curved lines ⌒ over groups of notes in music are called *slurs*. They are used to organize a piece into phrases. Learn to play your music in phrases just as you speak in sentences.

Teacher's Note: Additional finger numbers may be added if this book is being used for a beginner. However, numbers should be used sparingly so the student learns to read notes, *not* finger numbers.

2. SNUG AS A BUG IN A RUG

(Place hands in C major position as on page 6.)

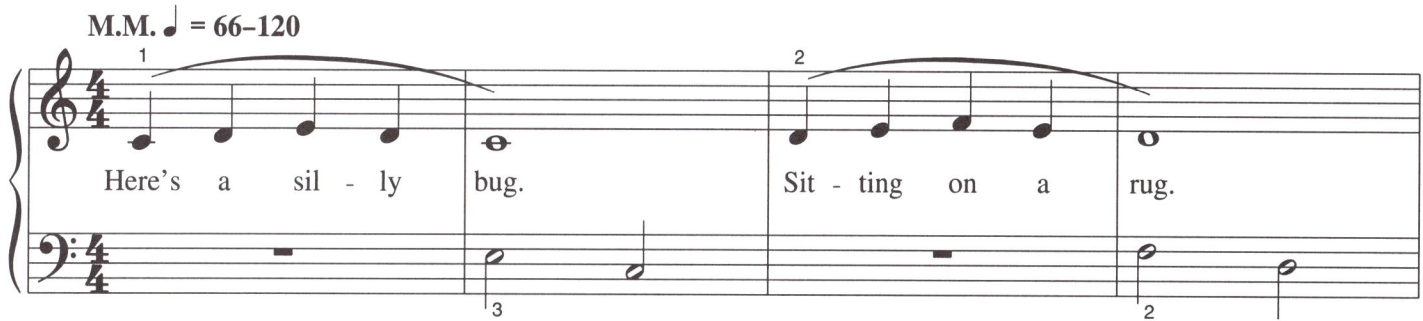

Here's a sil-ly bug. Sit-ting on a rug.

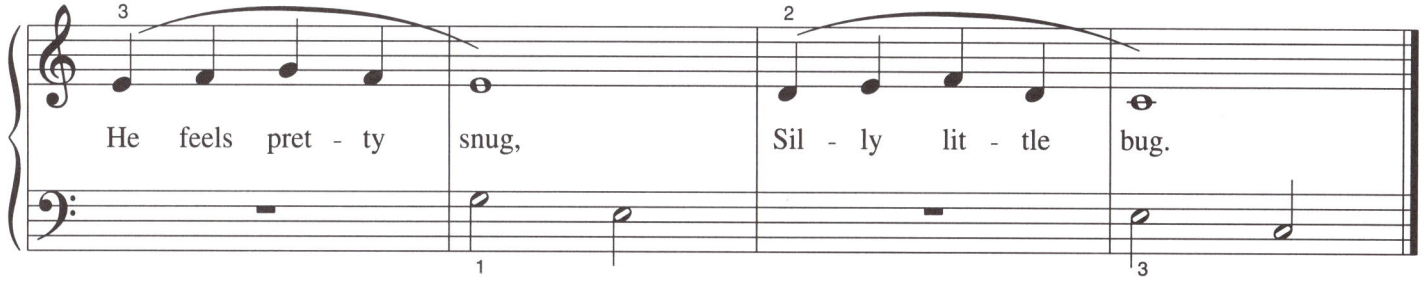

He feels pret-ty snug, Sil-ly lit-tle bug.

MUSIC AND POETRY

Music is like poetry. Both are made up of a series of similar phrases. A musical phrase is composed of a certain number of notes grouped into a melodic pattern. A poetical phrase consists of a certain number of syllables to a line.

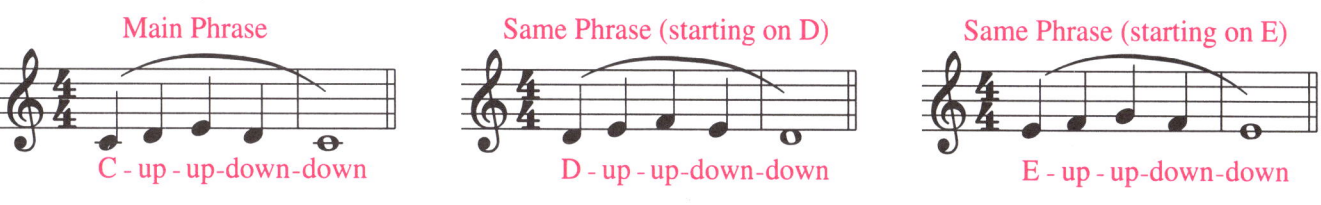

Main Phrase — C - up - up - down - down
Same Phrase (starting on D) — D - up - up - down - down
Same Phrase (starting on E) — E - up - up - down - down

As a preparatory drill, play this phrase starting on F, G, A and B. Then notice how "Snug As a Bug In a Rug" is built on this phrase.

Introducing eighth notes ♫. Two eighth notes equal one count.
One eighth note ♪ is half as long as a quarter note.

3. HANNAH FROM MONTANA

(C major hand position)

M.M. ♩ = 66–120

Once a young la - dy named Han - nah, Was in a flood in Mon - tan - a. She float - ed a - way, Her sis - ter, they say, Ac - com - pan - ied her on the pi - an - o.

HOW TO COUNT

Here are two rows of dots:

1 . . . .

2 . .. .

The first row is EVEN; the second row is uneven. When you count, your counts must be as *even* to your ears as the first row of dots is *even* to your eyes. Never count to your playing, but always PLAY TO YOUR COUNTING. In this piece and in every piece in 3/4 time always play your first count slightly louder:

1 2 3 1 2 3 etc.
>   >

4. CRUNCHY FLAKES

(C major hand position)

M.M. ♩ = 66–120

Crunch-y Flakes. Crunch-y Flakes. Give you what it takes.

They are ver-y good for you. And they're tas-ty too.

Crunch-y Flakes. Crunch-y Flakes. Give you what it takes.

They will make you big and strong. Health-y all day long.

THE METRONOME

The letters M.M. at the beginning of a piece stand for Maelzel's Metronome. Maelzel marketed the first widely used mechanical metronome. The numbers on the metronome indicate ticks per minute. Thus, if the metronome is set at 60, it will be ticking seconds.

The metronome enables you to hear the tempo the composer had in mind. It may also be helpful in learning to keep a steady beat. Avoid constant use of the metronome, otherwise your rhythm may tend to sound mechanical.

EL00166A

MUSICAL TERMS

Music writing began in Italy. Therefore Italian words are used to tell us how music is played. If each country used its own language it would be very confusing. Suppose Russia described its music in Russian, and Norway defined its music in Norwegian, etc., we would have to know far too many languages. Consequently all countries have adopted Italian terms for their music. If we know the Italian terms, we will understand how to play music of any country. There are several Italian terms used in "Swinging Along." Look up their meanings in the chart at the bottom of the next page. Then write the definitions on the dotted lines after each term in the music.

5. SWINGING ALONG

(C major hand position)

Giocoso
Adapted from Franz Behr

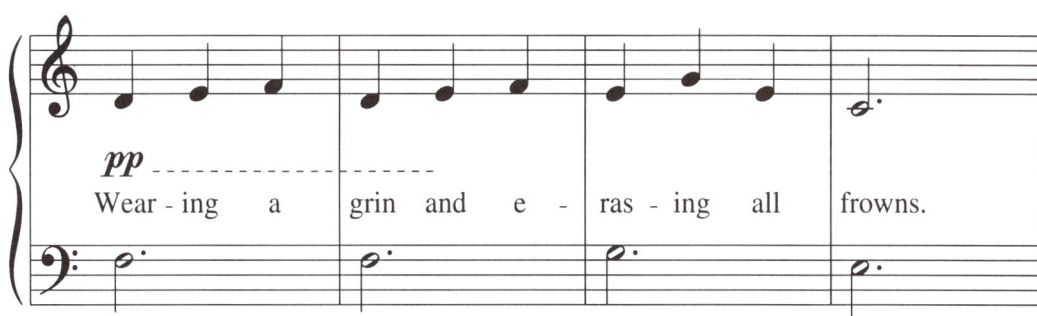

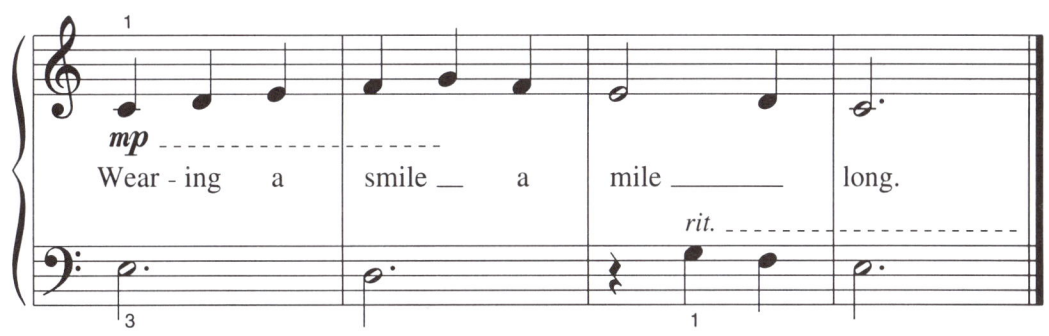

WORD MEANINGS THAT OCCUR IN "SWINGING ALONG"	
Giocoso	Joyfully; merrily
Legato	Connected; tones smoothly joined together
mf (Mezzo-forte)	Medium loud
p (Piano)	Soft
mp (Mezzo-piano)	Medium soft
f (Forte)	Loud
pp (Pianissimo)	Very soft
Rit. (Ritardando)	Becoming gradually slower

EL00166A

HALF STEPS AND WHOLE STEPS

(Memorize the following verse.)

A HALF STEP is from key to key,
With *no* key in between.
A WHOLE STEP always skips a key,
With *one* key in between.

Name the following steps: (Write W for Whole Step and H for Half Step)

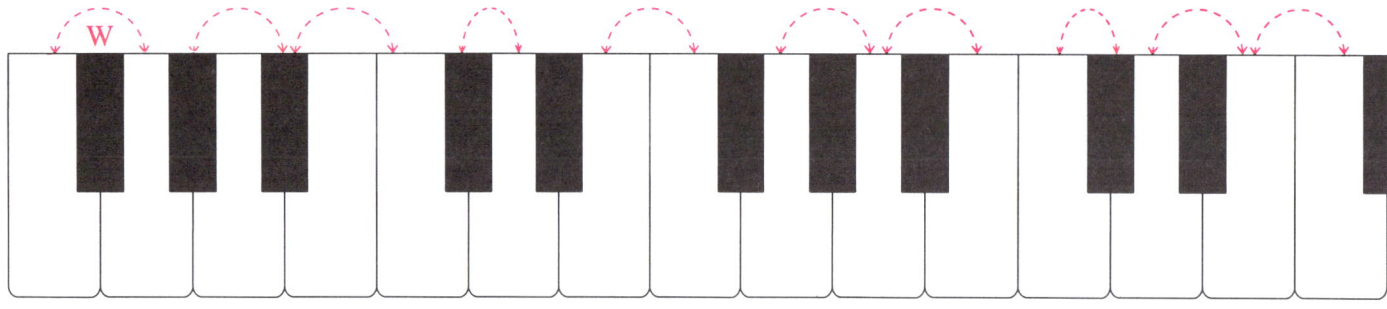

SHARPS AND FLATS AND NATURALS

The SHARP sign ♯ means to raise the key one half step.

The FLAT sign ♭ means to lower the key one half step.

The NATURAL sign ♮ means to go back to the white key.

Note: Each black key has two names. For example, F♯ (half step above F) and G♭ (half step below G) are the same key. In the dotted squares below, write the TWO names for each of the remaining black keys.

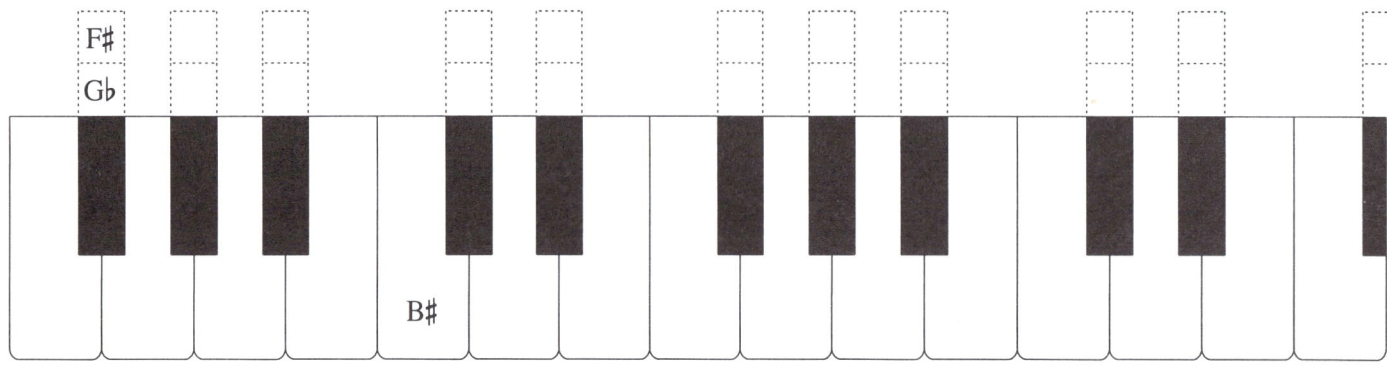

Sometimes a white key may actually be a sharp or flat. For example B♯. In raising B a half step, there is no black key to go to — so you borrow C and call it B♯. Write E♯, C♭ and F♭ on the above diagram.

ACCIDENTALS

The Sharp (♯), Flat (♭) and Natural (♮) signs which appear in a piece (other than in the key signature) are called *accidentals*. Watch out for them.

6. TICK-TACK-TOE

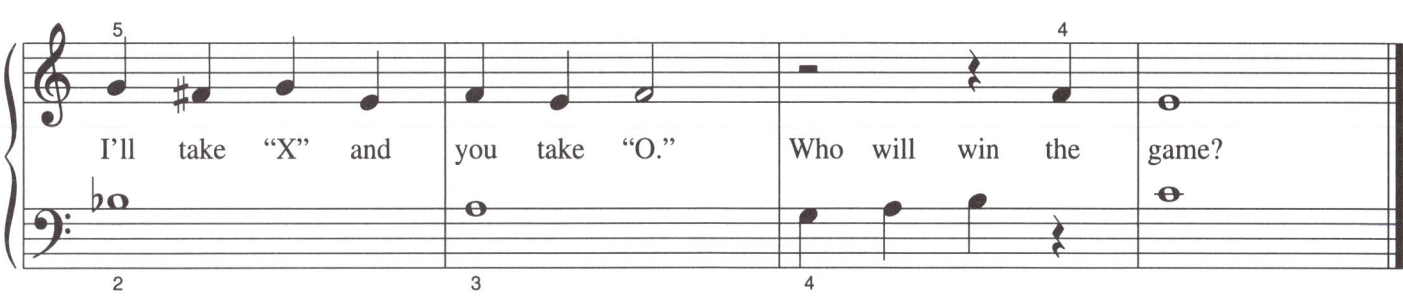

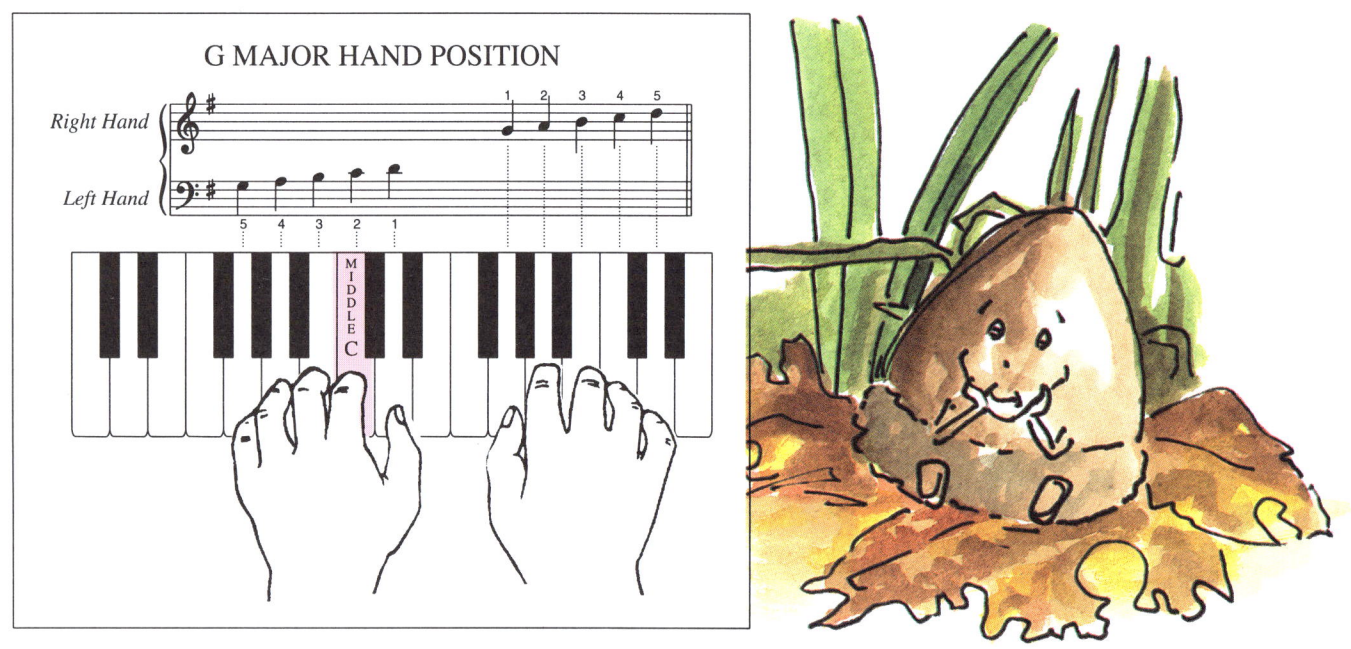

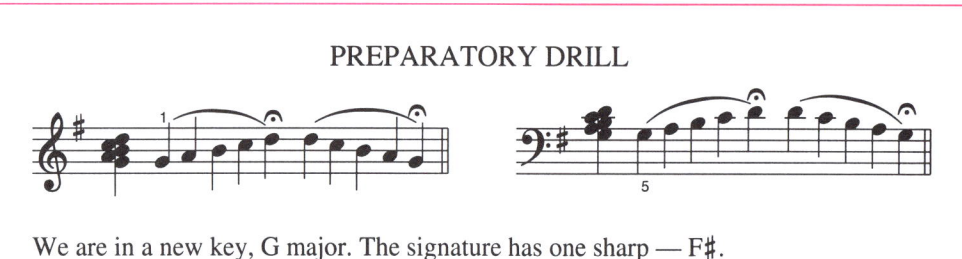

We are in a new key, G major. The signature has one sharp — F♯.

Place the hands over the keys shown in the hand position chart. Then play the preparatory drill several times. Keep your hands in this position when you play "A Nutty Song."

7. A NUTTY SONG

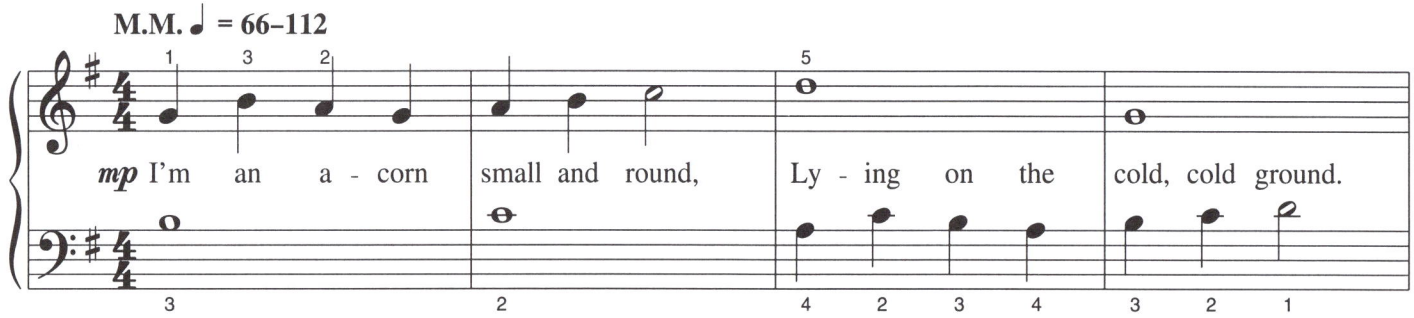

I'm an a-corn small and round, Ly-ing on the cold, cold ground.

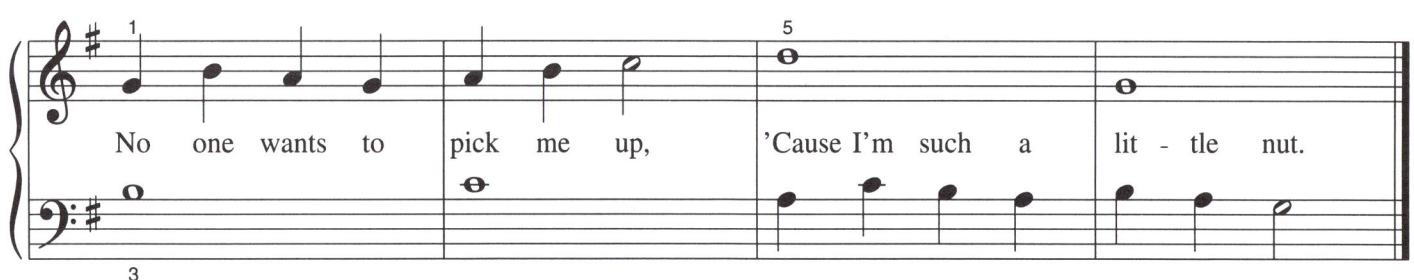

No one wants to pick me up, 'Cause I'm such a lit-tle nut.

HOW TO TRANSPOSE

To *transpose* means to play a piece in a different key. One way to transpose is by changing hand positions. For example, play "The Woodchuck" (page 6) in the key of G major. This is done by placing both hands in the G major hand position and using the fingering of the original key. Try transposing other C major pieces to G major.

You may also transpose G major pieces to C major. For example, "A Nutty Song" (page 14) may be transposed by using the C major hand position. Follow this same procedure with other keys as they are learned.

8. DOWN IN A COAL MINE

(G major hand position)

Down in a coal mine way un-der the ground.
Where gleams of sun-shine can nev-er be found.
Dig-ging black dia-monds the whole sea-son 'round.
Down in a coal mine way un-der the ground.

Watch for the new expression marks.

◁ (*crescendo*) means to grow louder.
▷ (*diminuendo*) means to grow softer.

A STORY ABOUT BEETHOVEN

This melody "Bells Are Ringing" is from Beethoven's Ninth and last symphony. The great music hall shook with applause when a chorus and orchestra finished performing it for the first time, but Beethoven sat with bowed head tapping time and worrying as to its acceptance. A friend turned his head so he could see the people clapping; Beethoven was deaf for his last 20 years, and never heard his own great symphony.

10. BELLS ARE RINGING

(G major hand position)

Adapted from Beethoven's Ninth Symphony (Choral)

Giocoso M.M. ♩ = 66–112

f Bells are ring-ing, Hearts are sing-ing, Hymns of love and life worth-while.

mp Can-dle light's a love-ly sight with sing-ers march-ing down the aisle.

All man-kind with one great mind u-nites in free and joy-ful song.

f Bells are ring-ing, Hearts are sing-ing, Hymns of love and life worth-while. *rit.*

Two Christmas Recital Suggestions

1. Have three boys dressed as the Three Wise Men play WE THREE KINGS OF ORIENT ARE (Specially arranged by John W. Schaum as a Piano Trio (One Piano — Six Hands) (PA00525)

2. For Piano Solo: O HOLY NIGHT (Cantique de Noël) Adolph Adam. Arranged by John W. Schaum in Key of C. Easy. (PA00508)

THE ARM PHRASING TOUCH

So that your piano playing may sound more artistic, the Arm Phrasing Touch is presented here. Curved lines ⌢ called slurs divide music into phrases. By observing the phrase marks properly, your playing will become expressive.

Finger is touching key.
Elbow is down at side.
Produce tone by raising elbow laterally.
Tone is made the moment the elbow starts moving gradually up.

Finger is touching key.
Tone is produced by continuing to move the elbow up.
Elbow lifts the finger slightly off the keys.

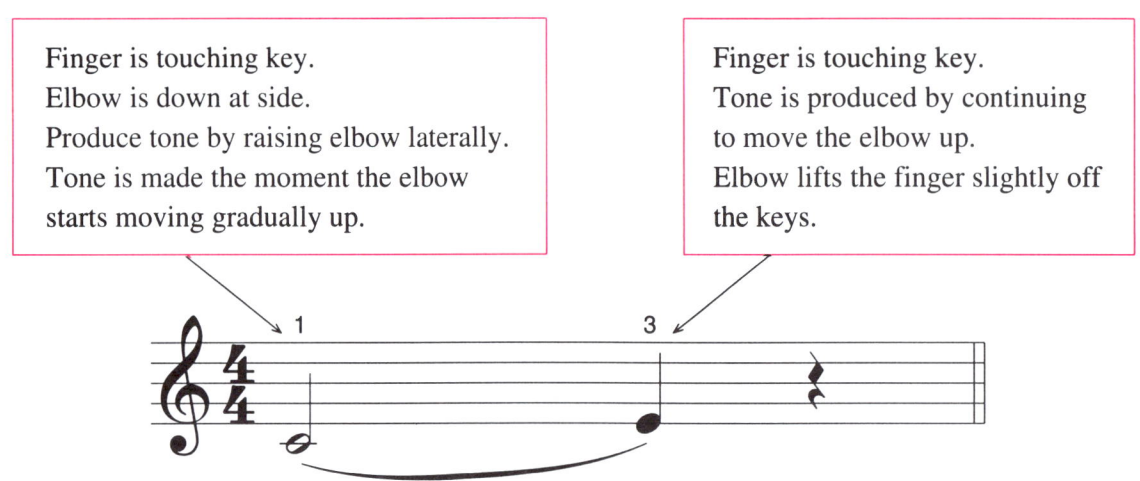

11. STEADY EDDIE

(Use the Arm Phrasing Touch.)

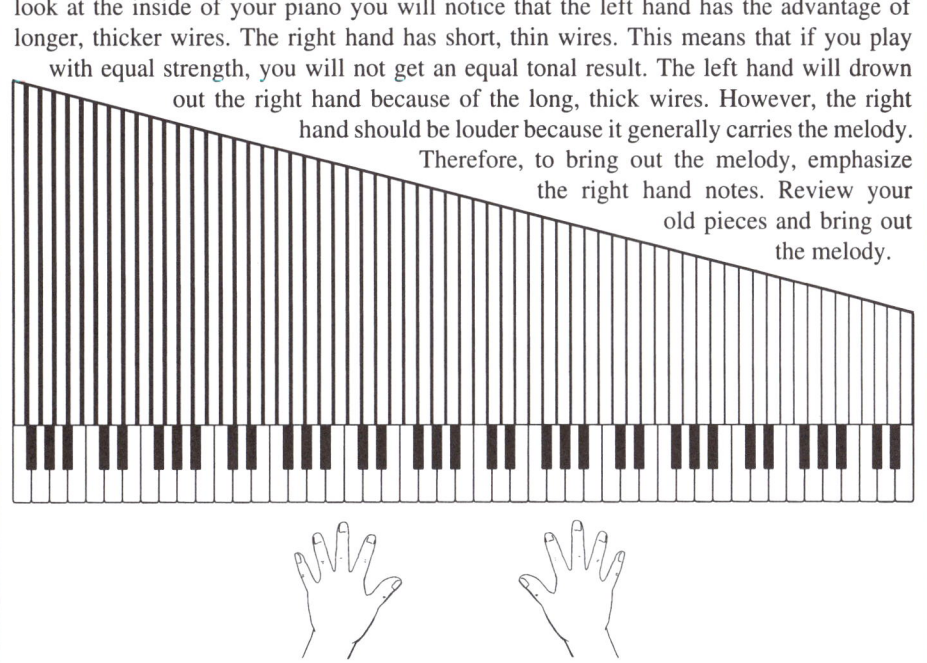

HOW TO BRING OUT THE MELODY

Notice the diagram below. The vertical lines represent the strings of the piano. If you look at the inside of your piano you will notice that the left hand has the advantage of longer, thicker wires. The right hand has short, thin wires. This means that if you play with equal strength, you will not get an equal tonal result. The left hand will drown out the right hand because of the long, thick wires. However, the right hand should be louder because it generally carries the melody. Therefore, to bring out the melody, emphasize the right hand notes. Review your old pieces and bring out the melody.

Left Hand   Right Hand

12. THE GOOFY GOPHER

(Use the Arm Phrasing Touch.)

Moderato means moderate speed.

Moderato M.M. ♩ = 72–116

Once there was a goof-y goph-er, Liv-ing

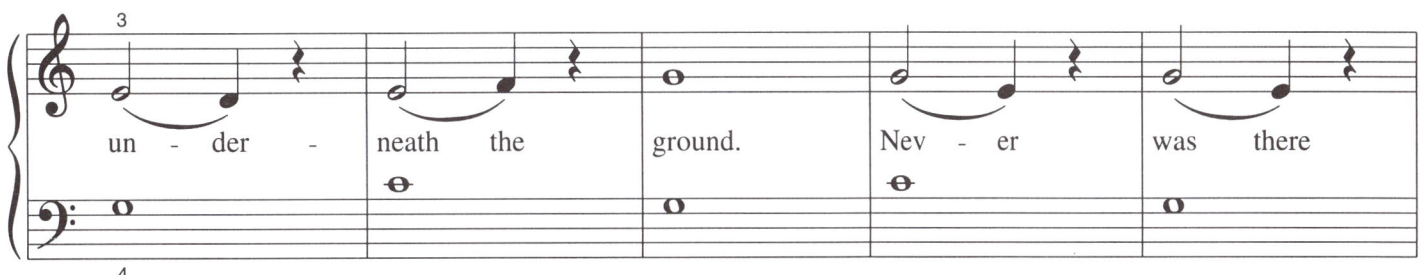

un-der-neath the ground. Nev-er was there

such a loaf-er, An-y-where else to be found.

EL00166A

SIGHT READING DRILLS

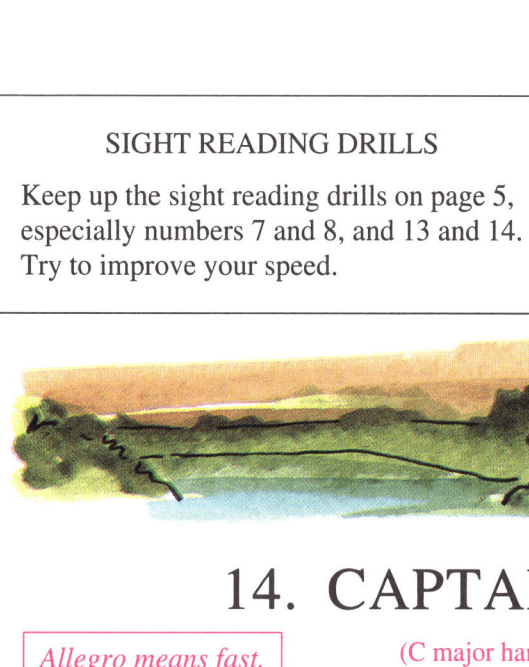

Keep up the sight reading drills on page 5, especially numbers 7 and 8, and 13 and 14. Try to improve your speed.

14. CAPTAIN SILVER

(C major hand position)

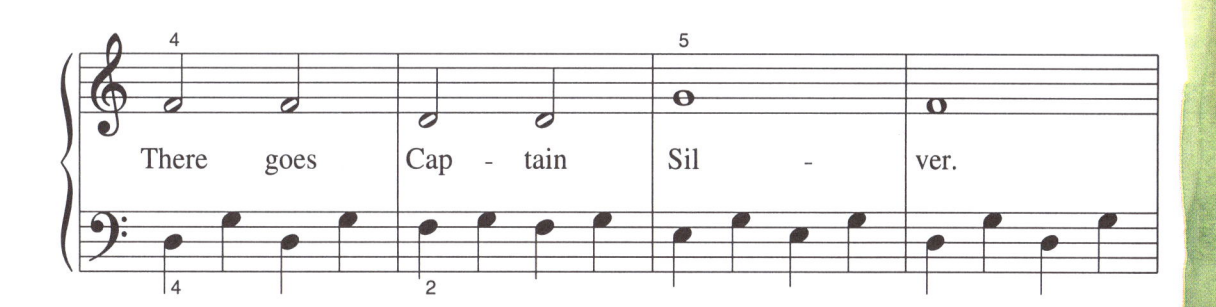

Allegro means fast.

Allegro M.M. ♩ = 120–160

Adapted from Jensen

f Hear those hors - es' hoofs on the trail.

There goes Cap - tain Sil - ver.

Chas - ing thieves who just stole the mail.

He'll put them in jail.

EL00166A

SCHAUM PIANO QUIZ NO. 1

DIRECTIONS: Below are twenty statements about music. If the statement is TRUE, mark T in the answer column. If a statement is FALSE, mark F.

All of the information has been presented in the preceding pages of this book. It is advisable to review these pages.

Date _____   Grade Marked _____

_____   _____
(Signature of Student)   (Signature of Teacher)

Answer Column

1. This is a tie. [musical notation] . . . . 1._____

2. This is a slur. [musical notation] . . . . 2._____

3. Slurs divide music into phrases. . . . . 3._____

4. In 3/4 time the second count should be accented. . . . . 4._____

5. The letters M.M. stand for Maelzel's Metronome. . . . . 5._____

6. All nations have adopted Spanish as their musical language. . . . . 6._____

7. Legato means to play in a smooth connected manner. . . . . 7._____

8. Forte (f) means to play softly. . . . . 8._____

9. Giocoso means to play slowly and sadly. . . . . 9._____

10. F♯ and G♭ are the same key on the piano. . . . . 10._____

11. A half step skips a key. . . . . 11._____

12. This is a sharp sign. (♮) . . . . 12._____

13. This is a flat sign. (♭) . . . . 13._____

14. The key of G has one sharp in the signature. . . . . 14._____

15. We can transpose by watching finger numbers. . . . . 15._____

16. We should never review our old pieces. . . . . 16._____

17. Beethoven was deaf in later life. . . . . 17._____

18. This sign means to grow softer. ⟩ . . . . 18._____

19. The sharps, flats, and naturals in a piece (excluding the key signature) are called accidentals. . . . . 19._____

20. Rit. (Ritardando) means to grow louder. . . . . 20._____

A NEW WAY TO TRANSPOSE

Another way to transpose is to raise all the tones one *half step*. See page 12 for an explanation of the half step. Practice "Jumping Beans" in two ways:

1. On white keys, as written.
2. On black keys, each note one half step higher.

Note: Play all the notes with *stems up* with the *right* hand, all the notes with *stems down* with the *left* hand. Both hands should use the third finger throughout the piece.

R.H. = Right Hand   L.H. = Left Hand

♩ ← Stem *up* (R.H.)   ← Stem *down* (L.H.)

15. JUMPING BEANS

Note: Right hand stays on F (or F♯) all the way through.

Allegro M.M. ♩ = 120–160

Down in Mex-i-co they have some ver-y fun-ny jump-ing beans that hop and wig-gle to and fro un-til they're all worn out. In these beans are ti-ny bugs that make for all the leaps and wig-gles. When the bugs die, then the beans can't jump or hop at all.

rit.

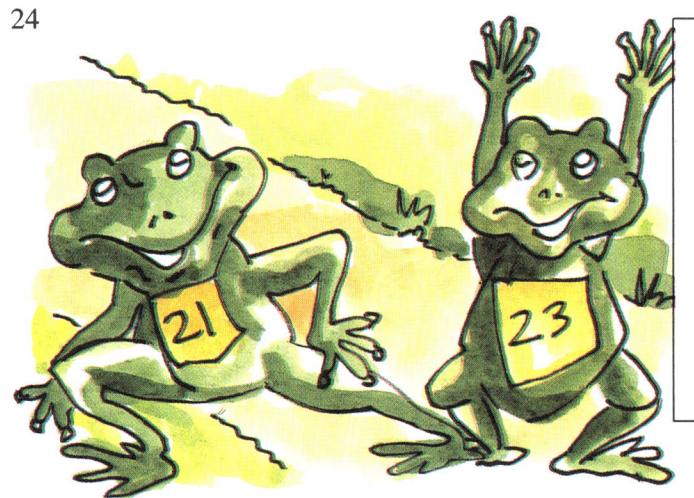

TRAINING THE FINGERS

Just as the athlete performs warm-up exercises, the pianist needs to get his fingers in condition. The following "Warm-Ups" give all the fingers in each hand a good workout.

Teacher's Note: The pupil should be told that each measure imitates the Main Phrase, going up one white key each time. Practice hands separately at first. Chords are also introduced.

16. WARM-UPS

(Can be taught by rote.)

Moderato M.M. ♩ = 60–108

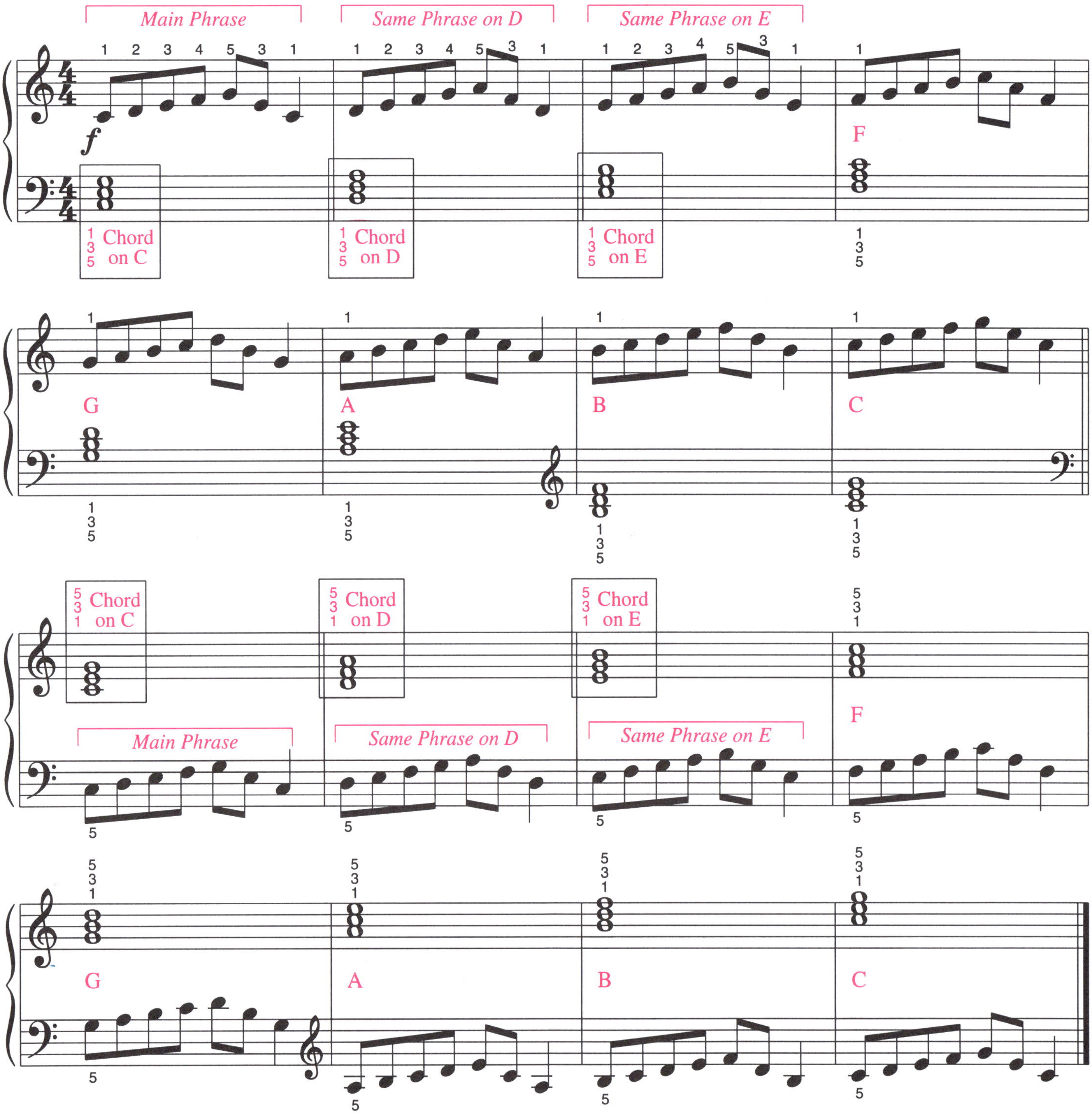

MEMORIZE THIS PIECE

This is a good piece to memorize for a recital. Note the left hand is the same throughout the piece.

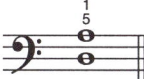

The right hand is in the following hand position.

This piece is in a minor mood. Minor pieces are mysterious and somewhat spooky.

17. THE SNAKE DANCE

Allegro M.M. ♩ = 120–160

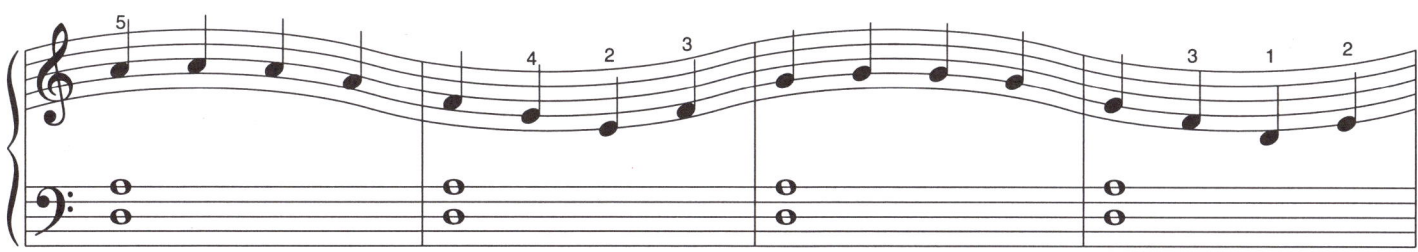

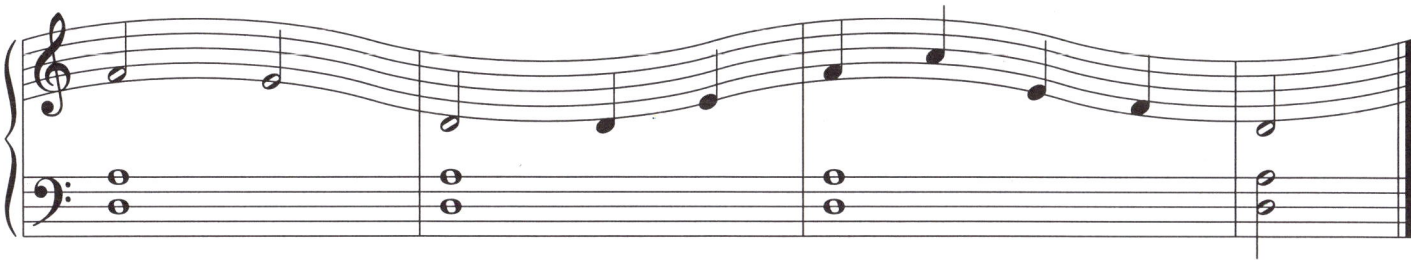

MAJOR SCALES

A *scale* consists of eight notes in alphabetical order beginning and ending on the same letter. These notes (called degrees) are numbered 1, 2, 3, 4, 5, 6, 7, 8.

A *major scale* is a series of whole steps and half steps. The half steps come between 3 and 4, and between 7 and 8. All other steps are whole steps.

MAJOR SCALE PATTERN

The eight notes of the *major scale* are arranged according to the following pattern:

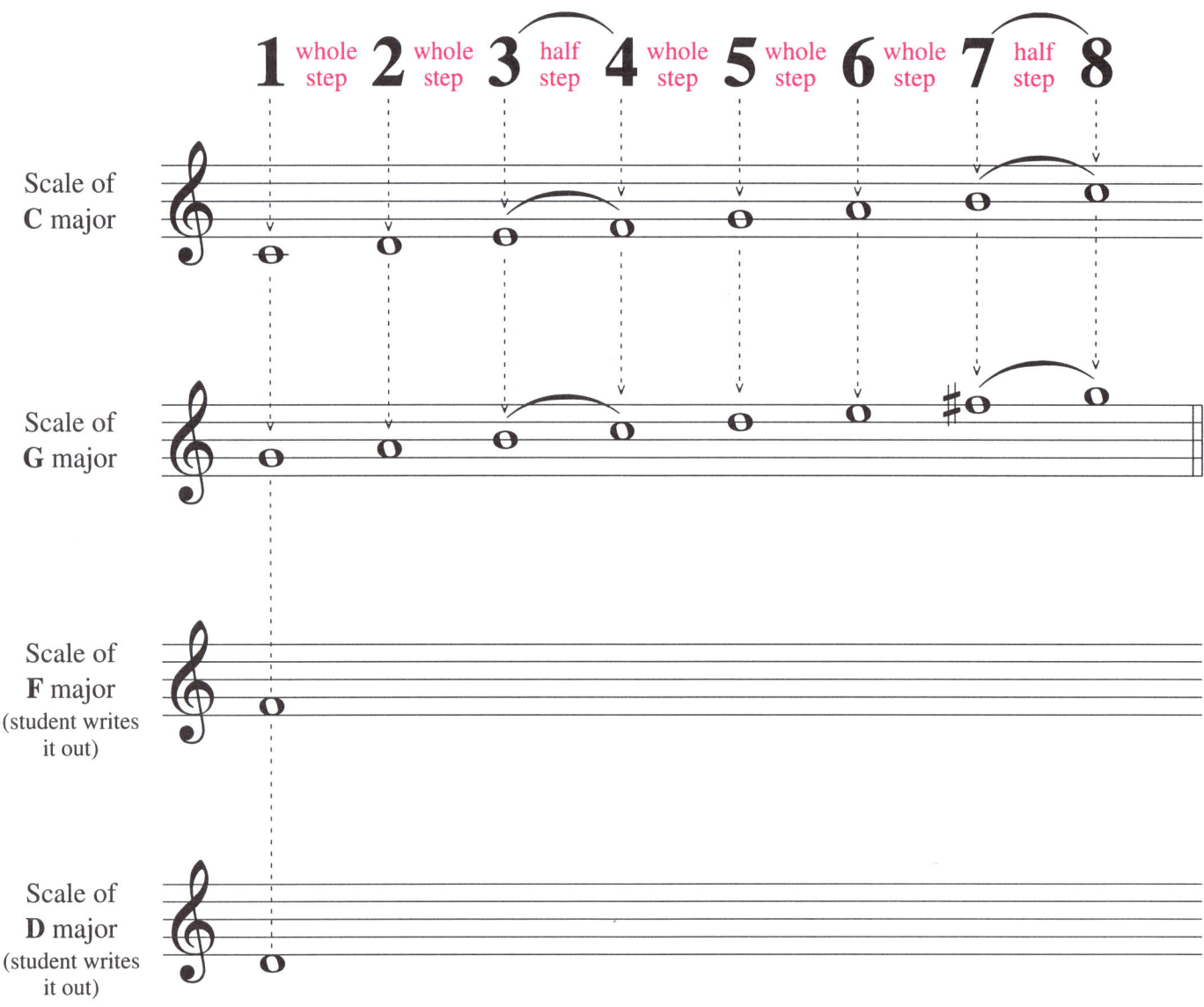

Teacher's Note: If desired, the teacher can have the pupil write out additional scales in a blank manuscript book.

SCALE OF C MAJOR

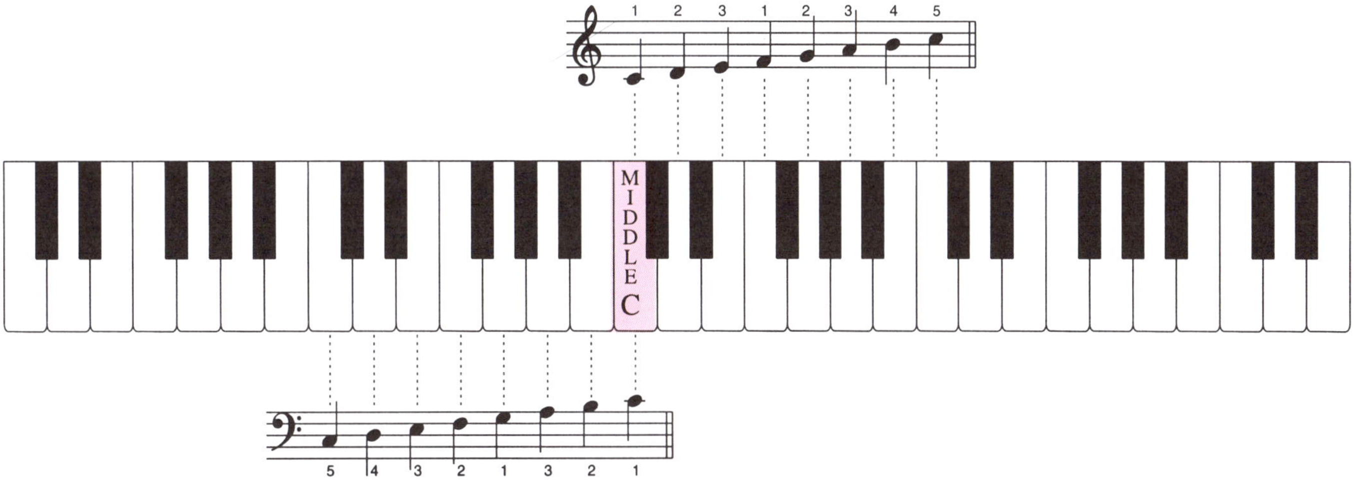

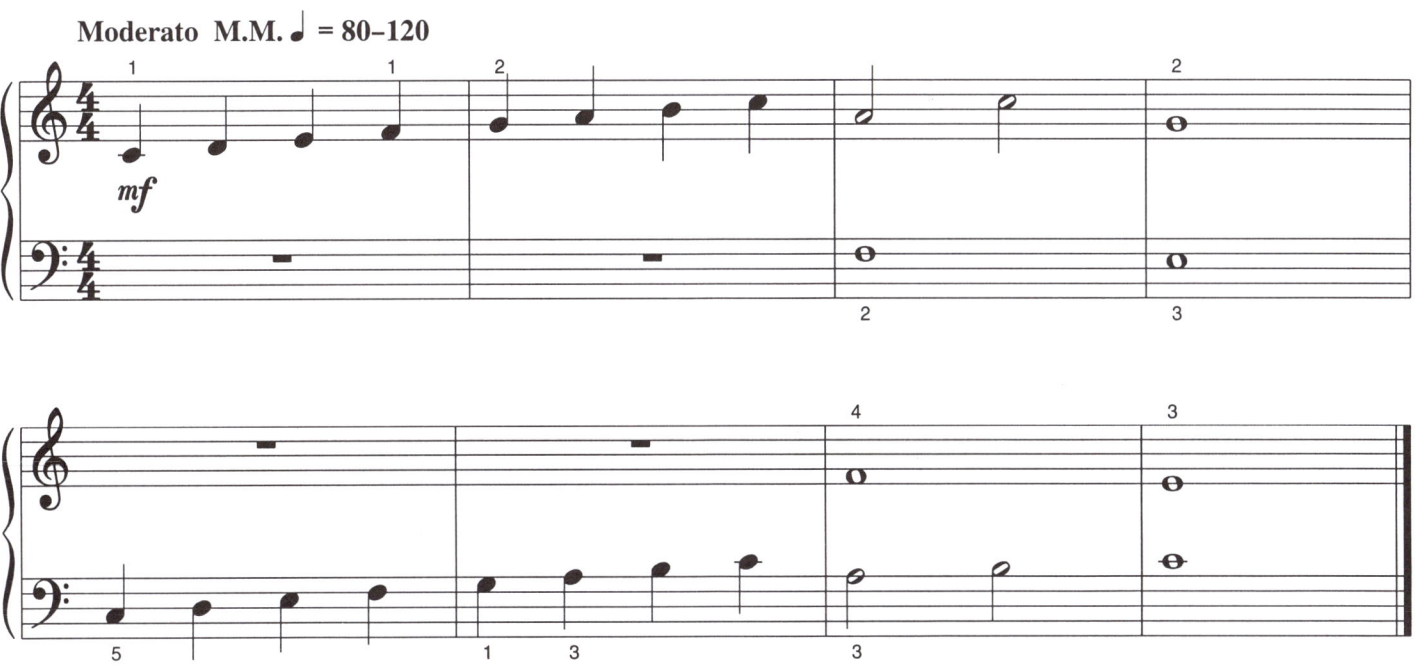

18. THE ESCALATOR

Moderato M.M. ♩ = 80–120

BROKEN CHORDS

Notice how the melody of "The Sphinx" is built on broken chords. See if you can find other broken chords in this piece and circle them.

19. THE SPHINX

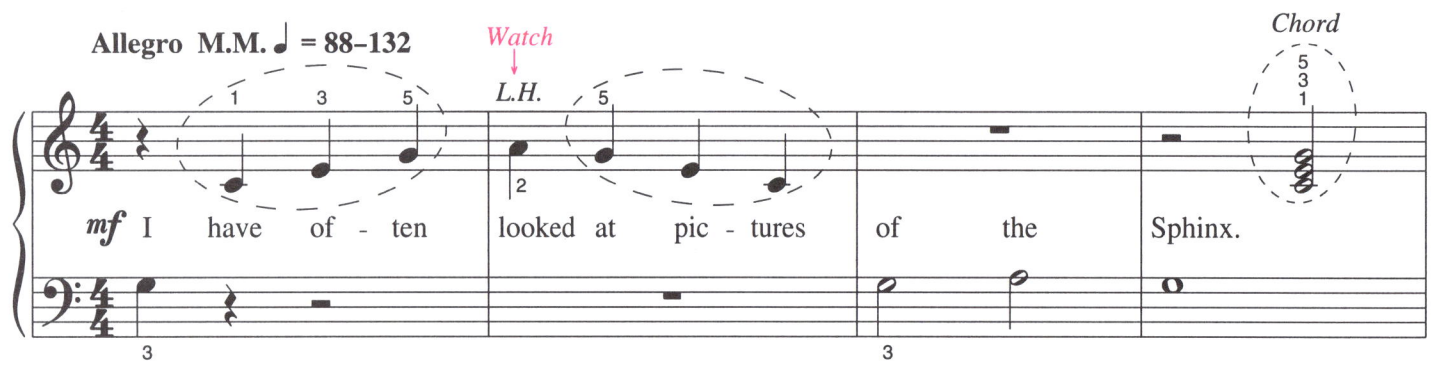

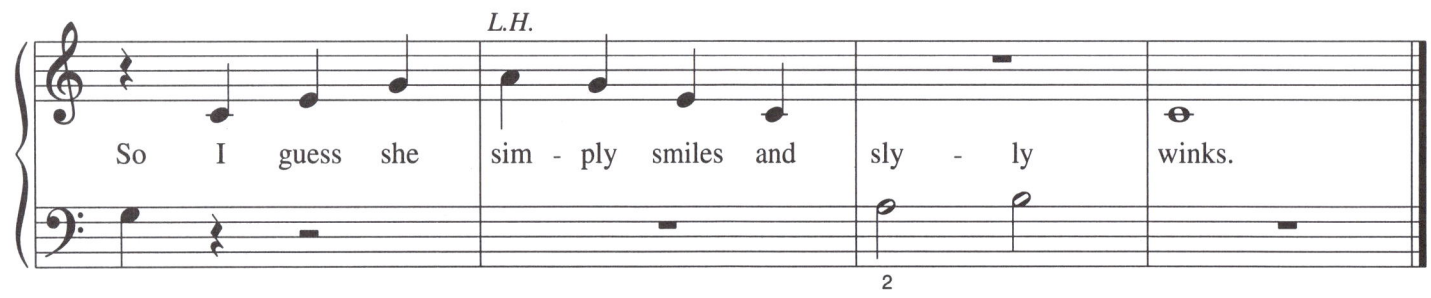

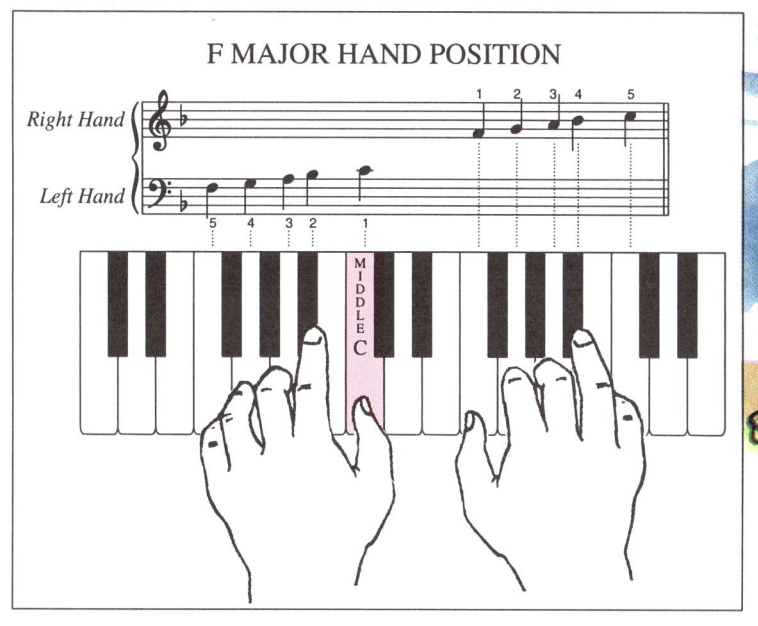

Place your hands in the new position shown above. Practice in bunches as before. Remember you are in the key of F major which has one flat (B♭) in the key signature. You are now ready to play "Tune of the Tuna Fish."

20. TUNE OF THE TUNA FISH

(Key of F major: one flat — B♭)

Moderato M.M. ♩ = 80–120

Tu - na fish! Tu - na fish! Sing a tune of Tu - na fish!
Tu - na fish! Tu - na fish! It's a fav - 'rite dish.
Ev - 'ry - bod - y likes it so. From New York to Ko - ko - mo.
Tu - na fish! Tu - na fish! It's a fav - 'rite dish.

EL00166A

HAND POSITION CHART
(Extension in right hand)

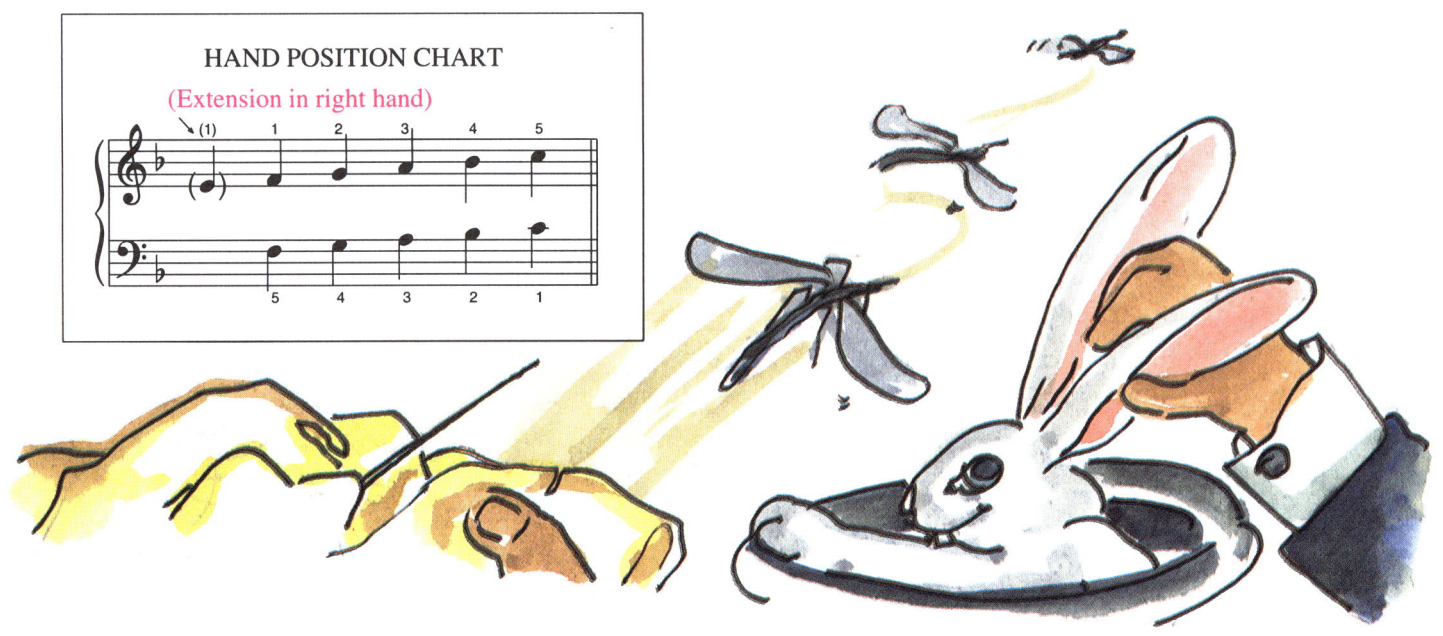

21. WHICH IS WITCH?

(Key of F major: one flat — B♭)

Moderato M.M. ♩ = 80–120

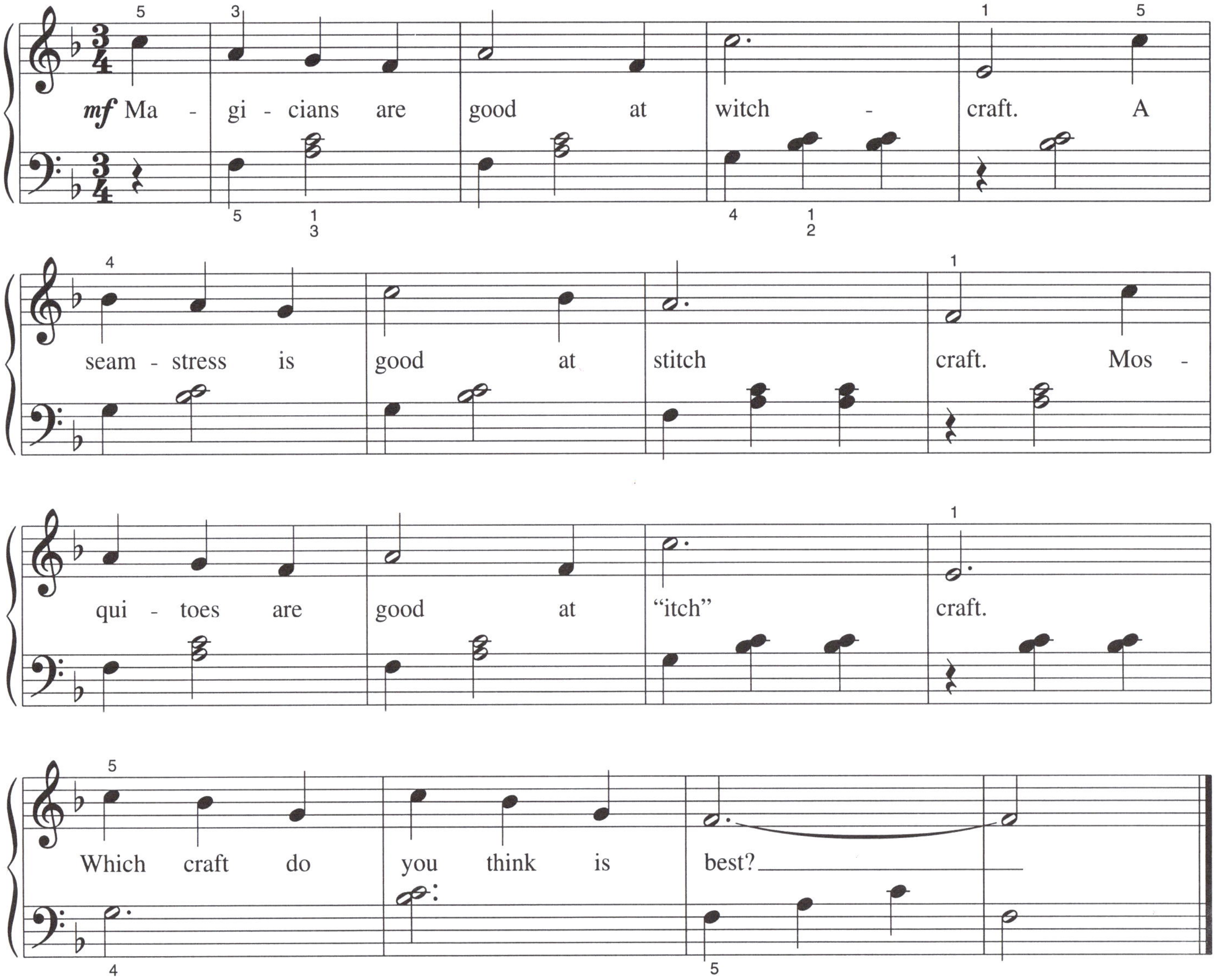

mf Ma - gi - cians are good at witch - craft. A
seam - stress is good at stitch craft. Mos -
qui - toes are good at "itch" craft.
Which craft do you think is best?

Now You Can Play

DOWN IN THE VALLEY (Key of F; $\frac{3}{4}$ time) arranged by John W. Schaum is a useful piece at this point. It gives the student additional experience in the key of F. (PA00561)

CONTRAST IN MUSIC

Music expresses many moods. Sometimes it excites us with its lively rhythms; other times it calms us with its quiet melodies. This famous song by Brahms is to be played softly and smoothly.

22. BRAHMS' LULLABY

(The right hand is in no particular hand position but rambles around. This will make the student read NOTES as well as FINGER NUMBERS.)

Largo means slowly.

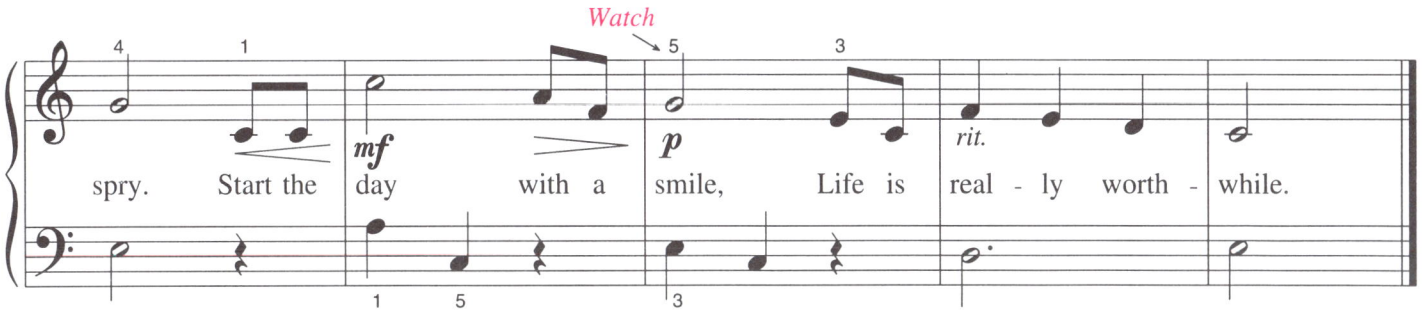

Practice the following left hand accompaniment patterns before you play the piece.

Teacher's Note: Explain repeat sign (:‖)

23. RIDING ON A MULE

(Key of G major: one sharp — F♯)

Moderato M.M. ♩ = 72–116

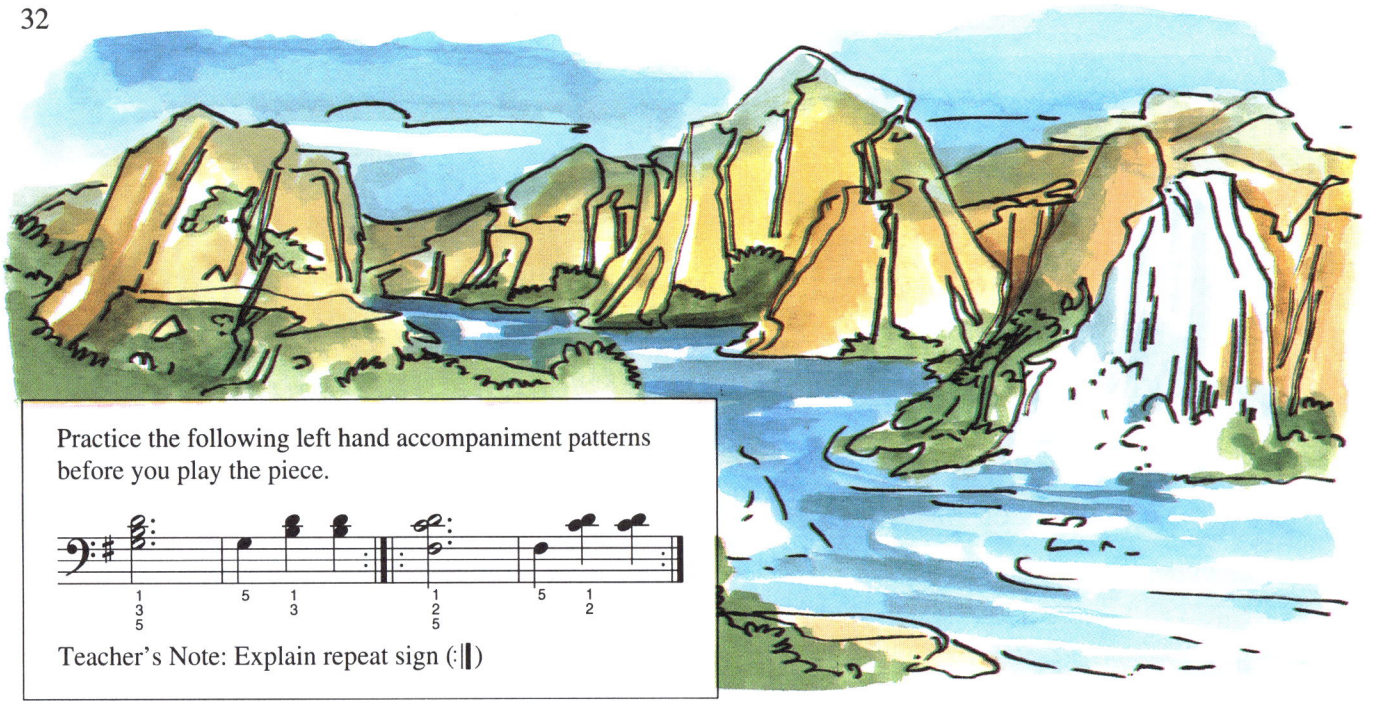

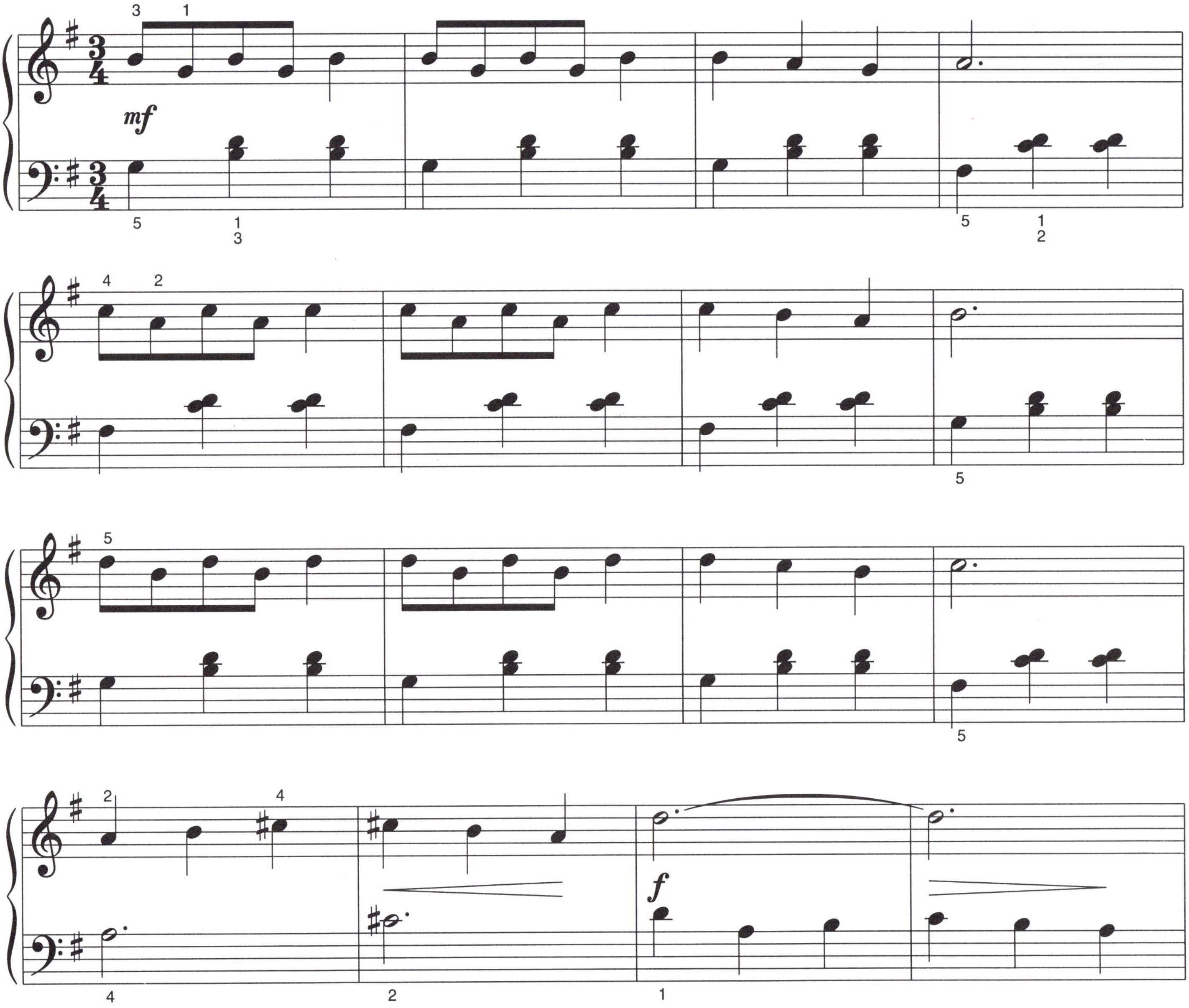

Place your hands in the D major hand position shown above.
Now you are all set to play "Cycles."

24. CYCLES

(Key of D major: two sharps — F♯ and C♯)

Andante M.M. ♩ = 66–104

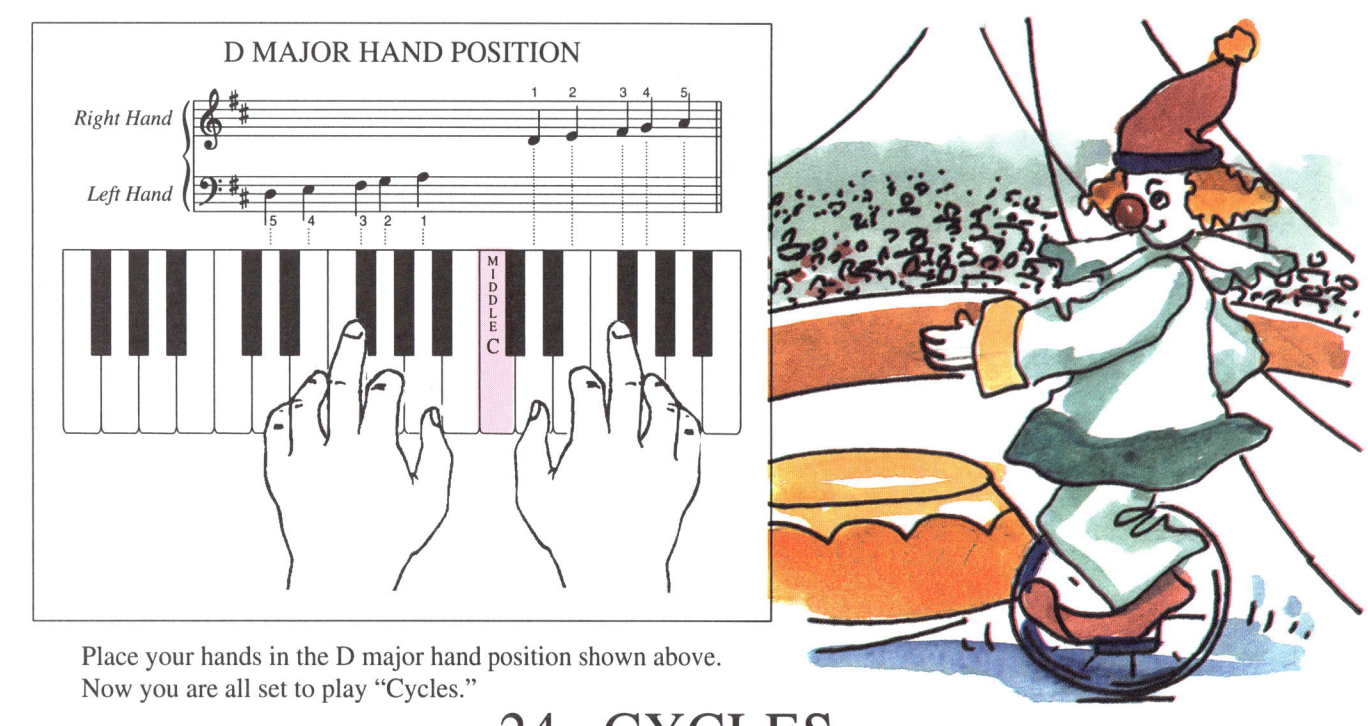

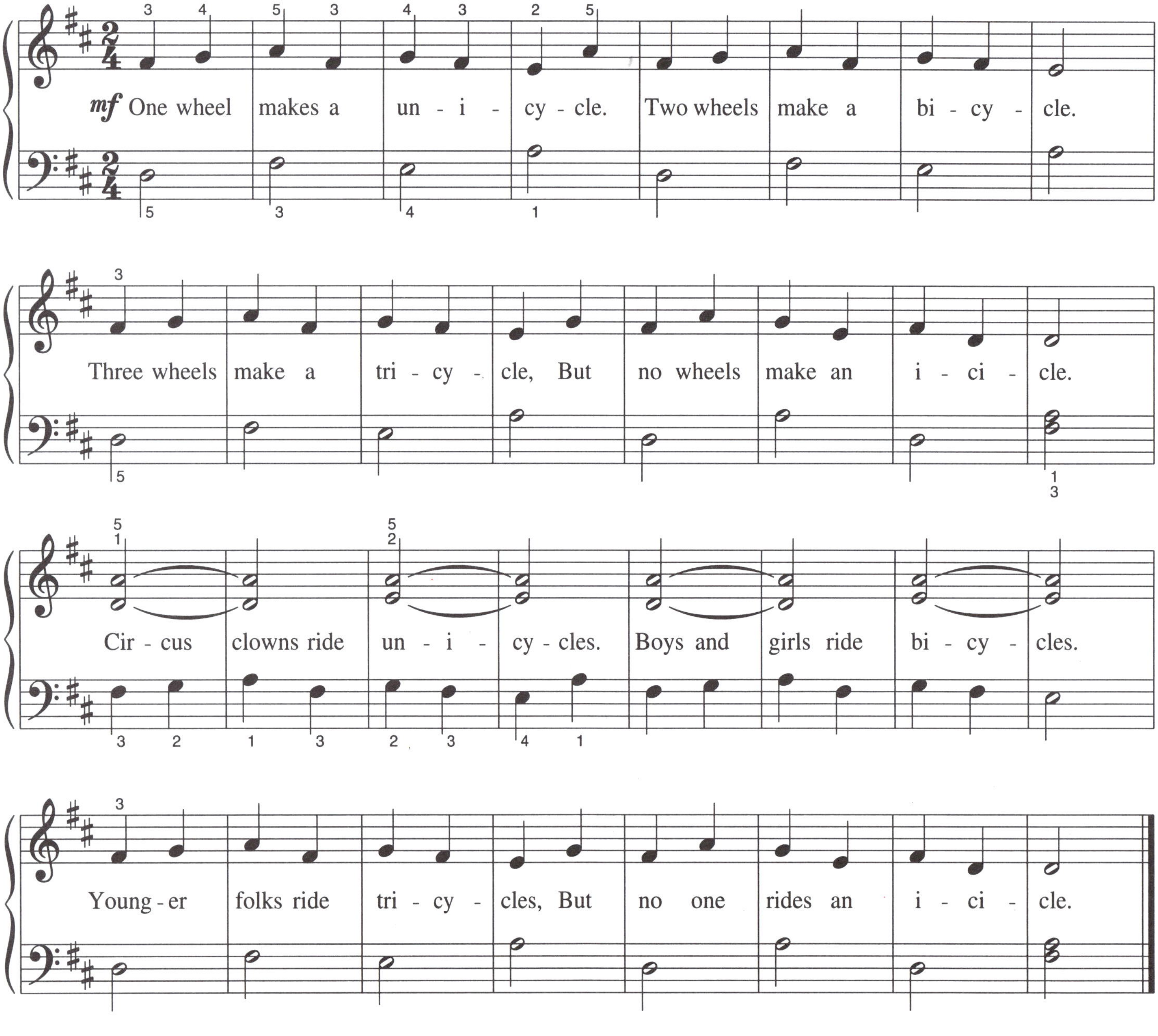

COMMON TIME

Sometimes you will not find a numerical time signature at the beginning of a piece, but instead a large letter **C**. This stands for COMMON TIME ($\frac{4}{4}$ time).

25. THE MOVIES

(Key of D major: two sharps — F♯ and C♯)

Allegro M.M. ♩ = 100–132

Extended Hand Position — *Regular 5 Finger Position*

At the mov-ie show, There are man-y thrill-ing fea-tures. Oh I love to go, To the new-est ac-tion show. In the eigh-teenth row, I can see just fine and dan-dy. Be it rain or snow, You will find me at the show.

EL00166A

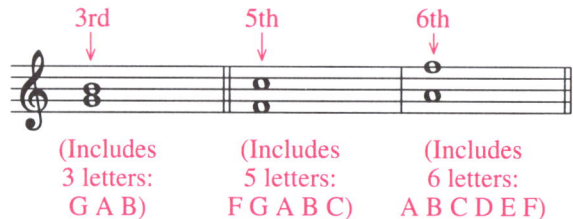

INTERVALS

An *interval* is the distance between two sounds. The number of an interval equals the number of letter names it includes. Study the following examples.

(Includes 3 letters: G A B)

(Includes 5 letters: F G A B C)

(Includes 6 letters: A B C D E F)

Draw circles around all the *thirds* in "At the Ice Cream Counter."

26. AT THE ICE CREAM COUNTER

(Key of G major: one sharp — F♯)

Moderato M.M. ♩ = 84–120

Adapted from Czerny

mp At the ice cream coun - ter,

Wait - ing for a treat.

Choc - 'late shake's my fav - 'rite,

Ice cream can't be beat.

EL00166A

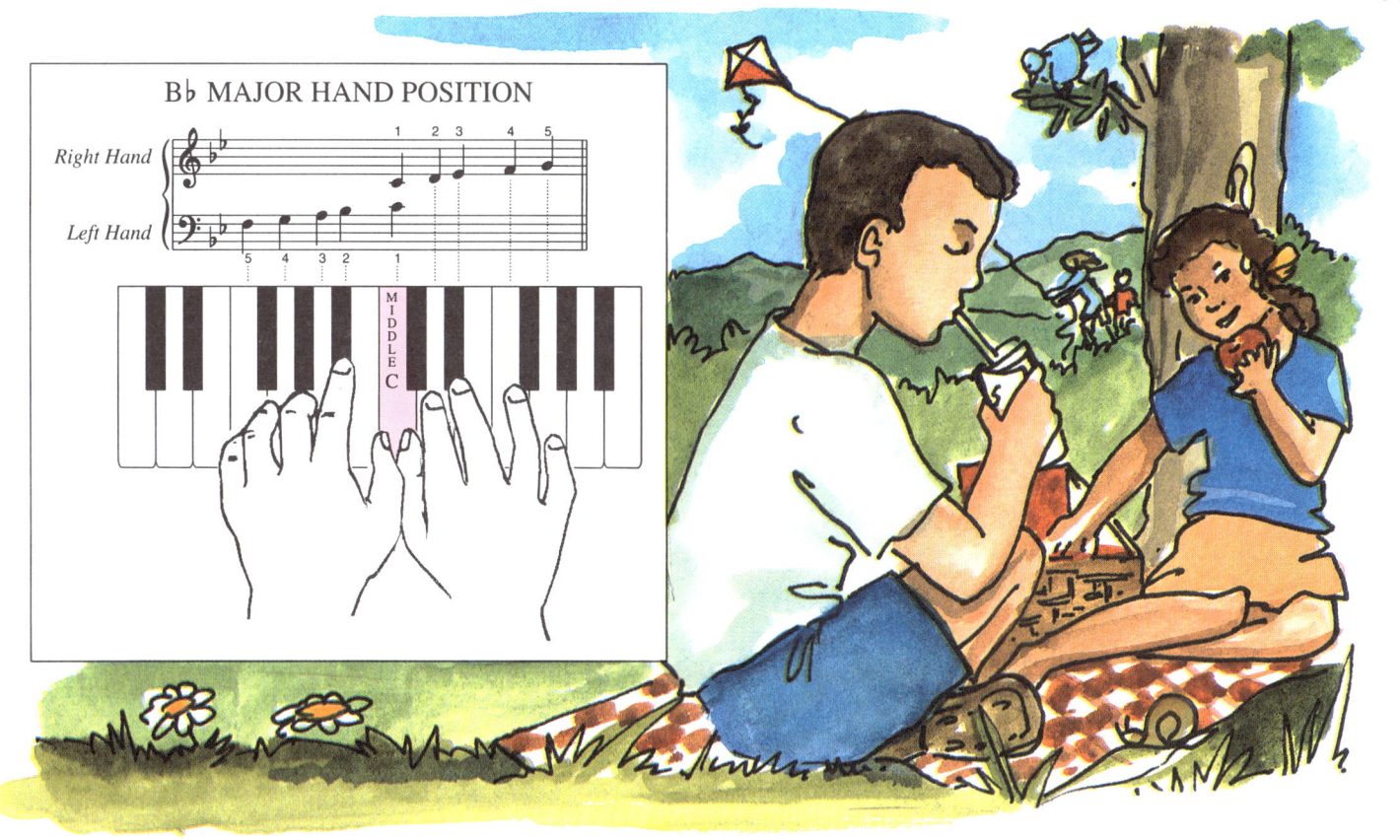

27. THE PICNIC
(Key of B♭ major: two flats — B♭ and E♭)

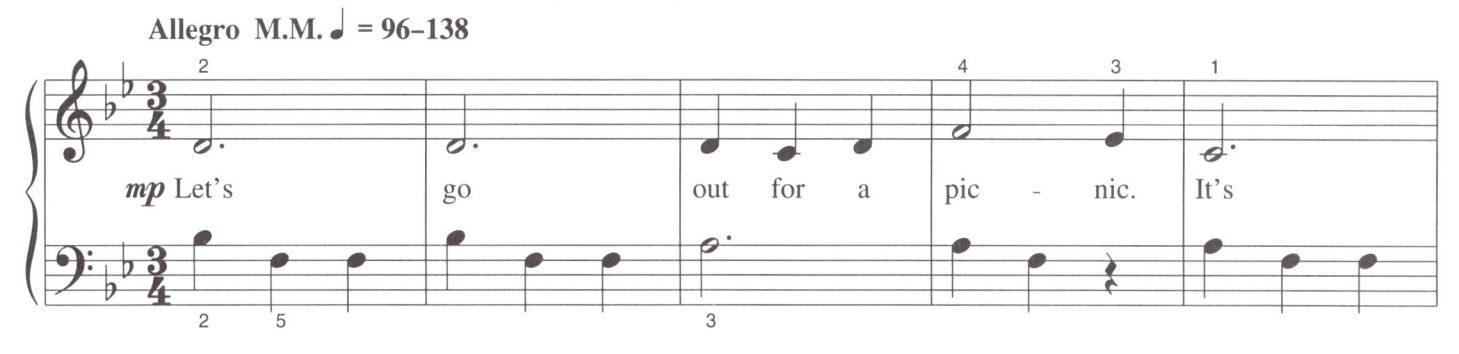

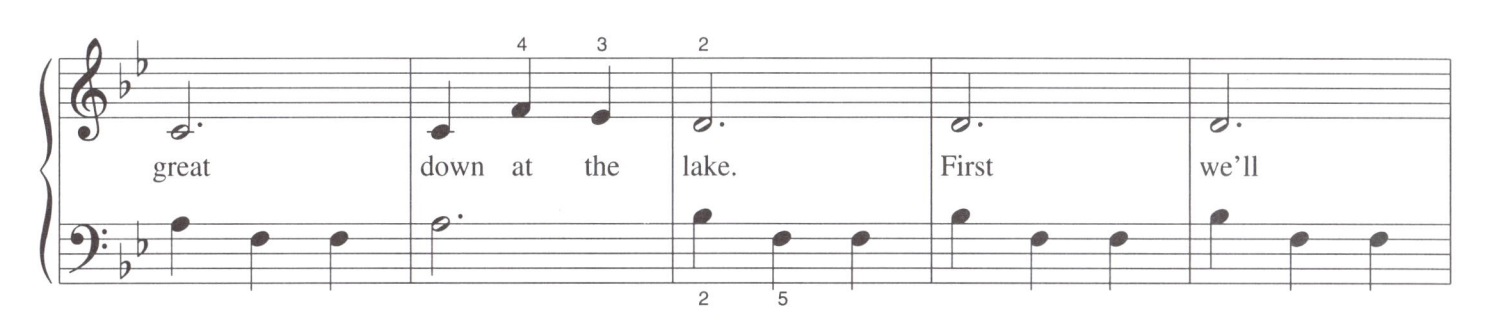

Allegro M.M. ♩ = 96–138

mp Let's go out for a pic - nic. It's great down at the lake. First we'll all go in swim - ming. Then we'll eat hot dogs and cake.

Left hand over — L.H.

THE PIANOFORTE

The full name of the instrument you are learning to play is *piano-forte*. Translated into English, it means *soft-loud*. So, you see, you are really learning to play the *soft-loud*. It all came about this way. On the early instruments that preceded the piano-forte, you couldn't play soft or loud. No matter how the keys were struck, the amount of tone was just the same. So naturally when they invented a keyboard that could be played soft or loud by the amount of pressure — they called it the *pianoforte* (*p-f*). But you may continue to call it *piano* for short.

28. THE LIFE GUARD

(Key of B♭ major: two flats — B♭ and E♭; same hand position as on page 37.)

ff fortissimo means very loud.

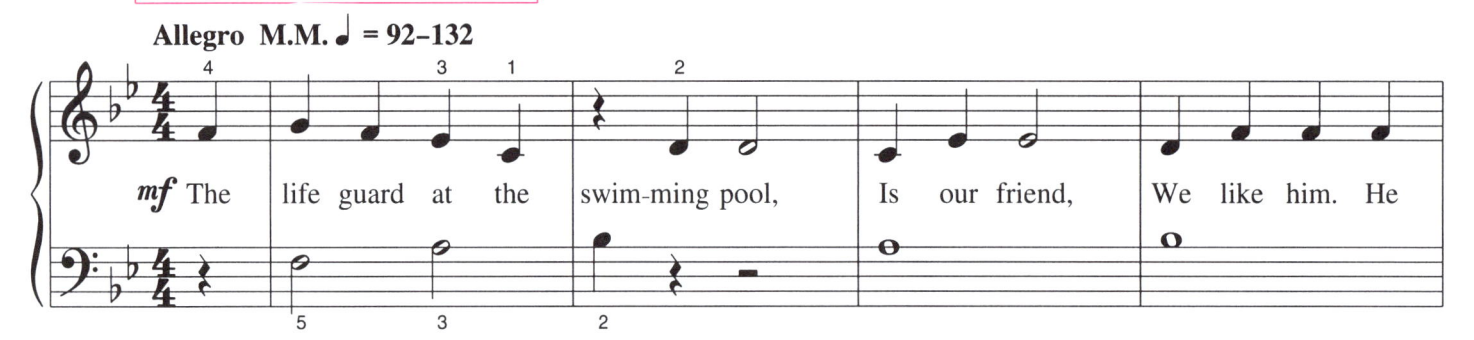

Allegro M.M. ♩ = 92–132

mf The life guard at the swim-ming pool, Is our friend, We like him. He

pp sees that we o - bey the rules, While we swim. The

mp life guard has to go to school, Learn to save peo - ples' lives. When

ff dan - ger comes he keeps his cool, At the pool.

PRACTICE SLOWLY

Slow practice keeps your playing clean and clear. Fast practice tends to make your playing messy. So, it's a good rule to always practice SLOWLY.

29. THE STEAM IRON
(STACCATO STUDY)

(Key of G major: one sharp — F#)

Moderato M.M. ♩ = 80–120

mp When you touch a hot steam i-ron, You let go as quick-ly as you can.

'Cause you'd sure-ly burn your fin-gers, And they'd be as brown as a pe-can.

When you play stac-ca-to notes, You lift your fin-gers quick-ly as you can.

Just pre-tend the keys are hot, You won't get burned be-cause you un-der-stand.

RECITAL PIECE

A MAJOR HAND POSITION

30. THE PET SHOP

(Key of A major: three sharps — F♯ C♯ and G♯)

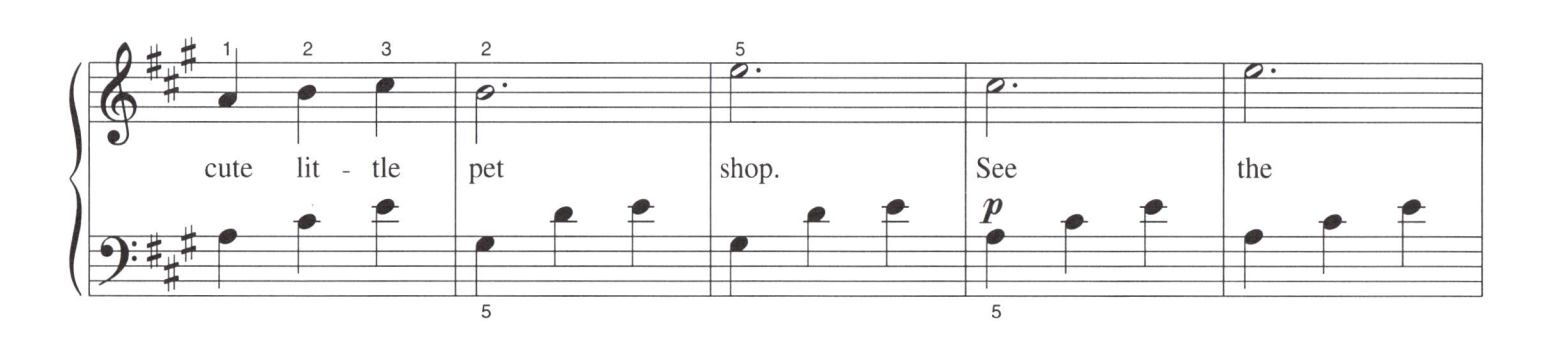

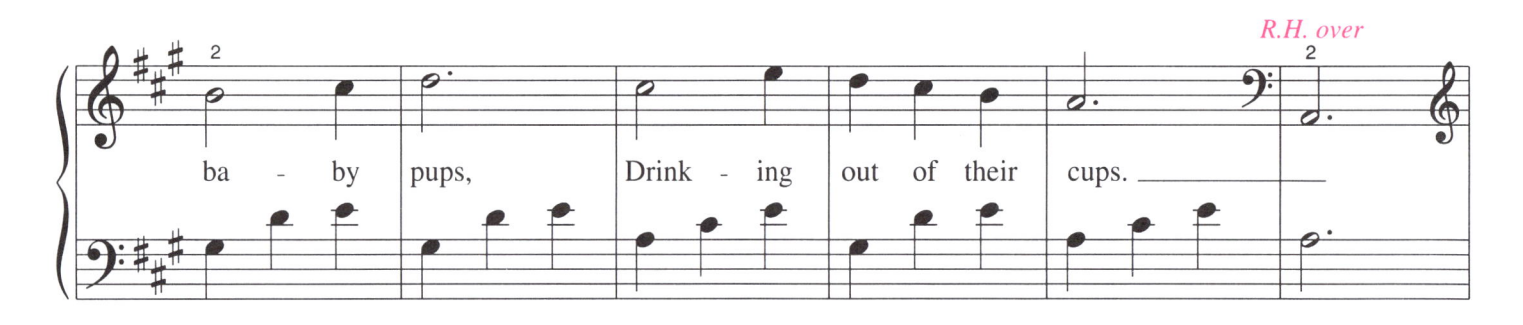

Moderato M.M. ♩ = 76–120

Adapted from Schubert

mf Let's look here and stop, At this cute lit-tle pet shop. See the ba-by pups, Drink-ing out of their cups.

p

R.H. over

f See! There's a ca - na - ry.

p Oh! Look at the mon - key.

mf Gold - fish, tur - tles too,

It's al - most like the zoo.

R.H. over

REPERTOIRE
(pronounced rĕp'er twôr)

This rather big word means the list of pieces you have practiced and have ready to perform. Concert pianists have very large repertoires (dozens of pieces). You should always have at least six pieces in your repertoire. This means to have six pieces ready to play at all times (by heart if possible).

31. THE RODEO

(Key of A major: three sharps — F♯, C♯ and G♯; same hand position as on page 40.)

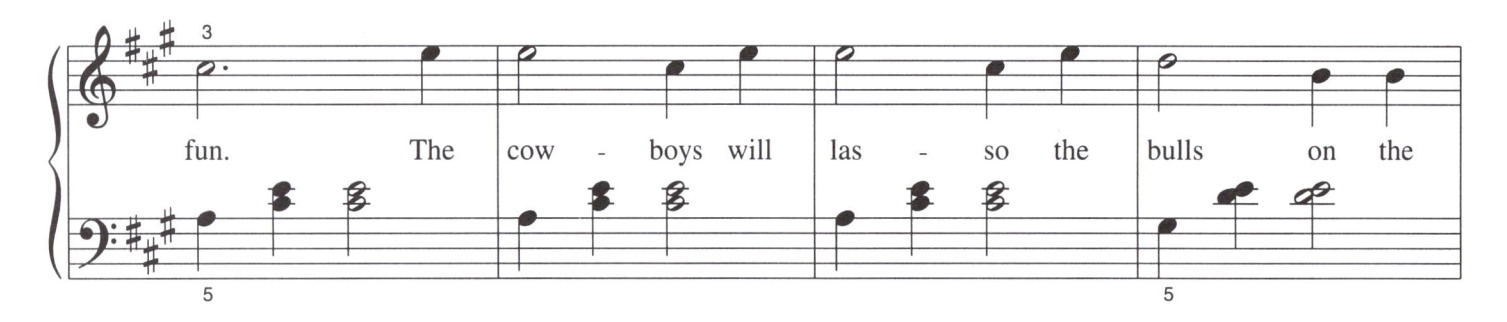

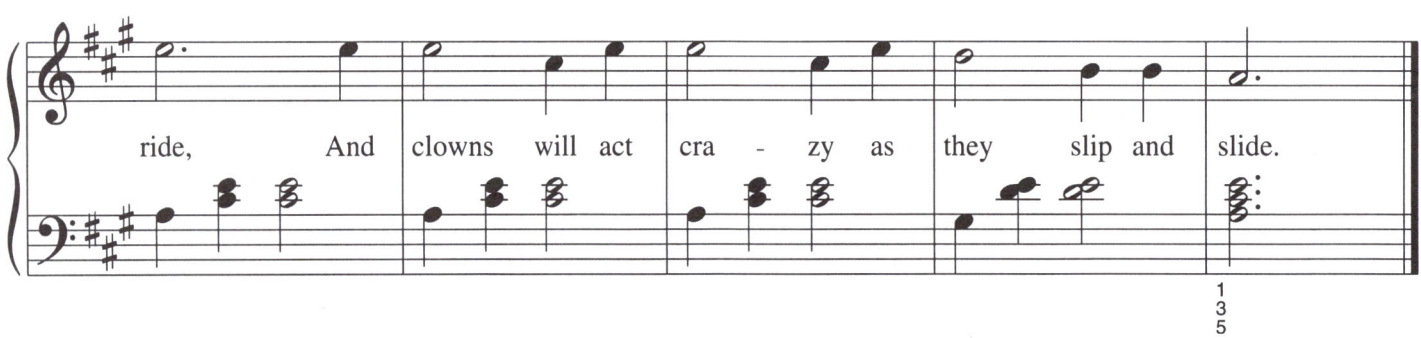

Allegro M.M. ♩ = 96–126

mf We'll see the ro - de - o and all have some fun. The cow - boys will las - so the bulls on the run. The cow - girls will do fan - cy stunts while they ride, And clowns will act cra - zy as they slip and slide.

THE DOTTED QUARTER NOTE

A dot after a note is equal to a note next lower in value; therefore the dot after a quarter note (♩) equals an eighth note (♪). The dotted quarter in 4/4 time is counted as follows:

♩. ♪ ♩. ♪
1 2 and 3 4 and

New L.H. Accompaniment Pattern

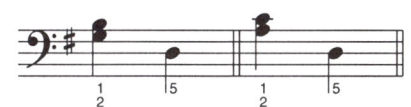

32. MOTORCYCLE COP

(Key of G major: one sharp — F#)

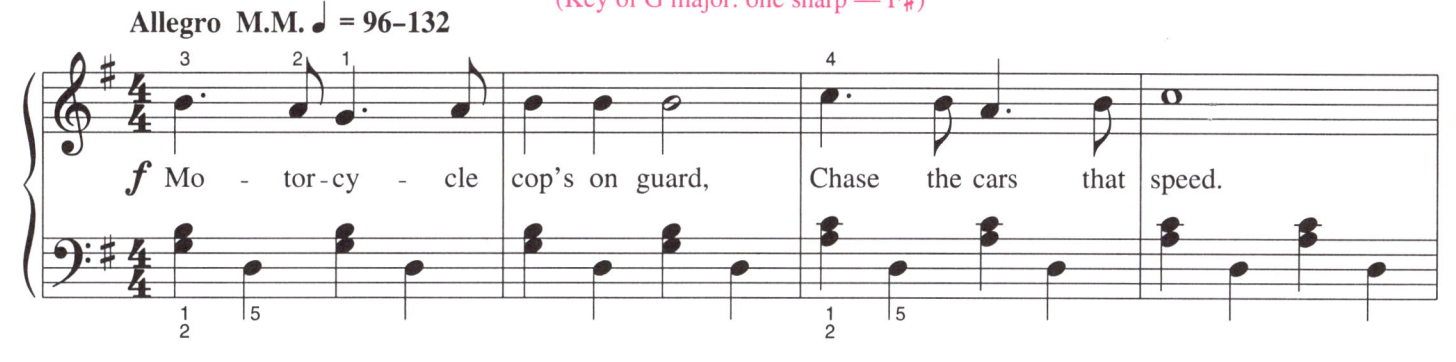

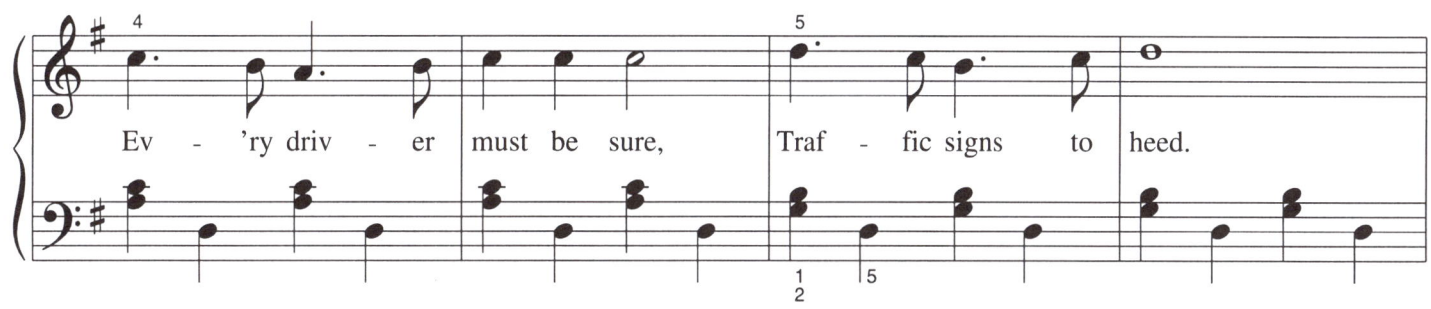

Allegro M.M. ♩ = 96–132

f Mo - tor - cy - cle cop's on guard, Chase the cars that speed.

Ev - 'ry driv - er must be sure, Traf - fic signs to heed.

Stop on red and go on green, That's the saf - est way.

Mo - tor - cy - cle cop's on guard, Laws we must o - bey.

Supplementary Solo

THE FOOTBALL GAME by John W. Schaum is a good "action" piece and should give the pupil a lot of enjoyment. (PA00510)

44

RIGHT HAND POSITION
(Key of A Major)

LEFT HAND CHORD PATTERNS

THE DOTTED QUARTER NOTE
in 3/4 time is counted as follows:

1 2 and 3

33. SCHUBERT'S WALTZ
(Key of A major: three sharps — F#, C# and G#)

Moderato M.M. ♩ = 80–120

mf Franz Schu-bert wrote six hun-dred songs or more. His "Ser-e-nade" is one we all a-dore. *p* This waltz that you're play-ing is one he wrote. *mf* Be sure you watch all dot-ted quar-ter notes.

EL00166A

REVERSIBLE MELODY
This piece can be played from either end.
Play it right side up; then play it upside down.
Place hands in the following position.

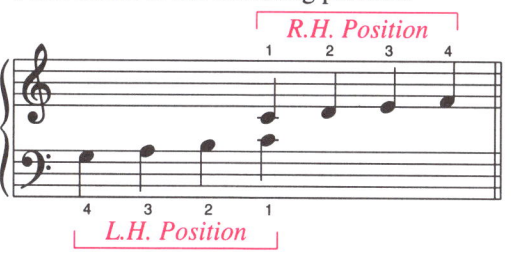

R.H. Position
L.H. Position

34. A MUSICAL TRICK
(Any way you look at it, it's a good tune.)

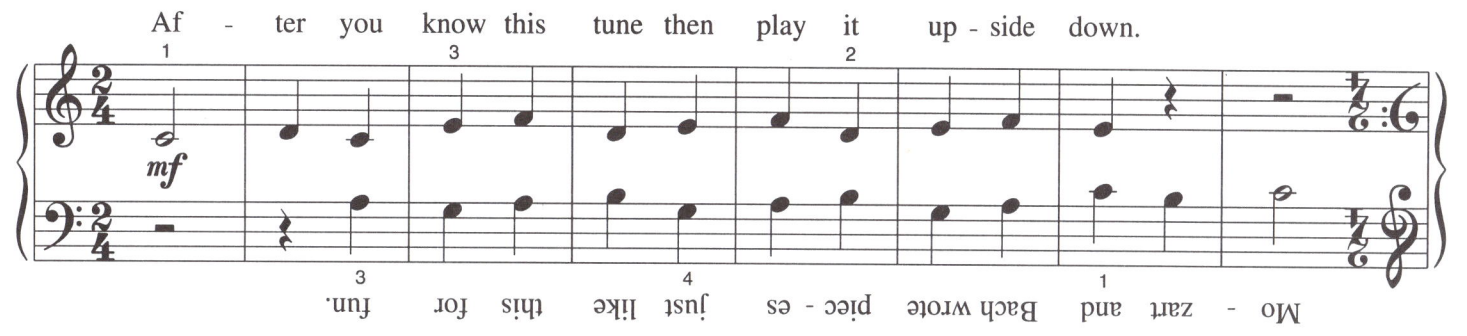

Andante M.M. ♩ = 72–104

After you know this tune then play it up-side down.

(upside-down text:) Mo-zart and Bach wrote piec-es just like this for fun.

(upside-down text:) 34. A MUSICAL TRICK
(Keep hands in same position as before.)

THE CHEERLEADER
B♭ Major Hand Position

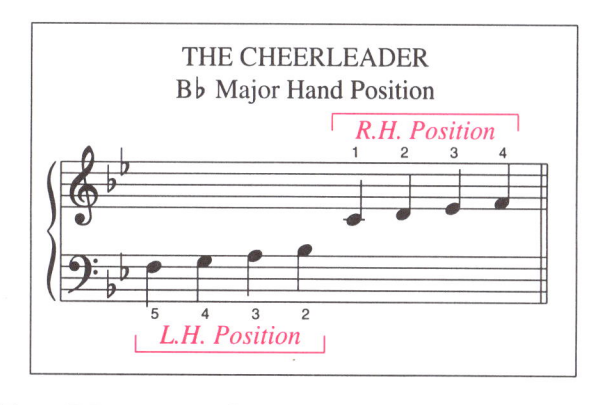

R.H. Position
L.H. Position

35. THE CHEERLEADER

Andante M.M. ♩ = 60–84   (Key of B♭ Major: two flats — B♭ and E♭)

f Come let's give the team three cheers. Hip - Hoo - ray! U - Rah - Rah!

Ev - 'ry - one must per - se - vere. So we'll win the game.

EL00166A

CHANGING KEYS

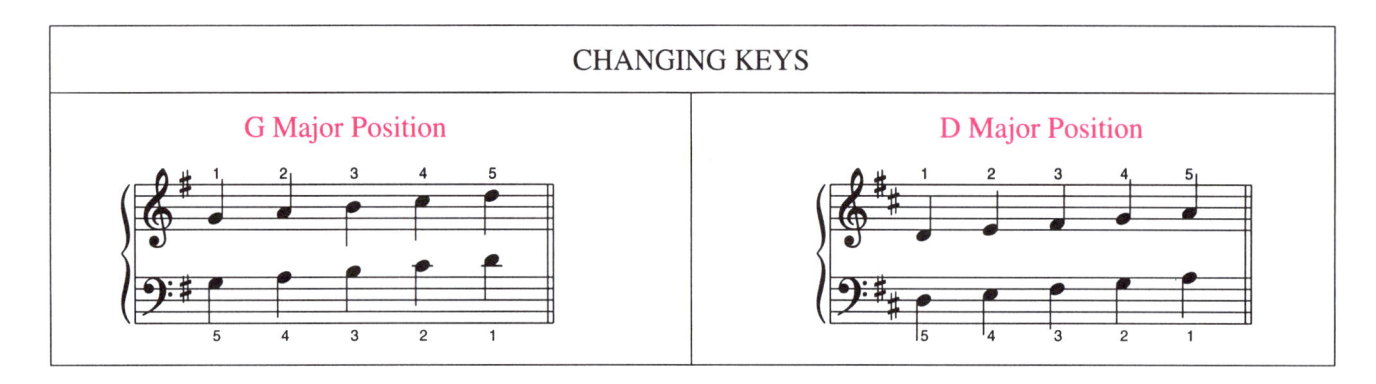

G Major Position

D Major Position

36. BIRTHDAY GREETINGS
(See footnote)

Moderato M.M. ♩ = 72–104

f Hap-py birth-day, dear Moth-er, Hap-py birth-day to you. *mp* Hap-py
G Major Position

birth-day, dear Moth-er, Hap-py birth-day to you.

f Hap-py birth-day, dear Fa-ther, Hap-py birth-day to you. *mp* Hap-py
D Major Position

birth-day, dear Fa-ther, Hap-py birth-day to you.

Note: TRUE BLUE LADY (A Tribute to Mother) Piano Solo in C major by John W. Schaum is an excellent piece for the pupil to learn as a surprise for mother. It is appropriate not only for her birthday, but for Mother's Day, and other holidays. (PA00560)

SCHAUM PIANO QUIZ NO. 2

DIRECTIONS: Below are twenty statements about music. If the statement is TRUE, mark T in the answer column. If the statement is FALSE, mark F.

All of the information has been presented in the preceding pages of this book. It is advisable to review these pages.

Date _____   Grade Marked _____

_____   _____
(Signature of Student)   (Signature of Teacher)

Answer Column

1. One way to transpose is to raise all the tones a half step. . . . . 1. _____

2. This [chord notation] is a chord. . . . . 2. _____

3. Pianists and athletes do not need exercise. . . . . 3. _____

4. Minor pieces are happy and cheerful. . . . . 4. _____

5. This [broken chord notation] is a broken chord. . . . . 5. _____

6. In a major scale the half steps come between 2 and 3, and 6 and 7. . . . 6. _____

7. The signature for the key of C major is one sharp. . . . . 7. _____

8. The signature for the key of F major is one flat (B♭). . . . . 8. _____

9. Some music is calm and other music is lively. . . . . 9. _____

10. Largo means cheerful. . . . . 10. _____

11. Two sharps in the signature indicate the key of D major. . . . . 11. _____

12. This sign [bass clef] stands for common time. . . . . 12. _____

13. This interval [notation] is a 4th. 13. _____

14. This interval [notation] is a 6th. 14. _____

15. The key of B♭ major has two flats (B♭ and E♭). . . . . 15. _____

16. If one *f* means forte, then two *ff*'s mean eighty. . . . . 16. _____

17. Pianoforte is the full name for the piano. . . . . 17. _____

18. Pianists should always practice fast. . . . . 18. _____

19. The three sharps in the key of A major are A♯, D♯ and B♯. . . . . . . 19. _____

20. The dot after a quarter note (♩.) is worth an eighth note (♪). . . . . 20. _____

Certificate

of

Promotion

This announces that

_____

has successfully completed the
John W. Schaum
Piano Course – A-Book
and is now ready to begin the
John W. Schaum
Piano Course – B-Book

_____ Teacher

Date _____